Dedication

For every soul who forgot their wings… and remembered. This book is dedicated to every woman who ever tried to change her colors just to survive; who contorted herself into silence; who folded herself up and made herself smaller for love, work, or other people's boxes. And doubted the brilliance of her own light. To the ones who encountered chameleons disguised as love, opportunity, or even family.

May you remember:

- ➤ Their camouflage was never your truth.
- ➤ This is for you - the survivor, the light bringer,
- ➤ The butterfly in bloom.

Chameleons & Butterflies

Volari Morgan

Printed & Published in Hiram, GA of the United States of America by
Joy Glow Media

Identifiers: LCCN: 2025922214 (print) | ISBN: 979-8-9999071-0-3 (paperback)
979-8-9999071-1-0 (ebook) | 979-8-9999071-8-9 (hardback)

Cover & Interior design: Volari Morgan

First Edition, 2025
This book is intended to provide encouragement, inspiration, and personal reflection. The author and publisher make no guarantees regarding outcomes and disclaim liability for any loss or damage incurred as a result of the use of this material.

For more information, visit: www.myjoyglows.com

The First Founders
of The Flight

To those who held this dream in their hands before the ink had even dried, you are the wind that lifted these wings. Your faith in these pages, before the world had seen them, is a gift I will never take lightly.

You didn't just purchase a book, you invested in a vision, you said "yes" to a story still in the making. Each of your names is etched into the heart of this work, like constellations guiding me through the dark.

Because of you, these wings stretch wider. Thank you for being my first support, the proof that when a story is ready to be told, there will always be souls ready to hear it

.

Bonnie Taylor Natelege Hemmings

Vlademir McKeithen Andra Hoxie Ingrid Underwood

Victoria Brannan Cami Barnes Victor Brannan

Khani Morgan DeneQuia Able Nikki Thompson

Adrienne Carthon-Lyons Xavier Morgan

Nefetari Murphy Bahji Varner Nikol Davis

Sarah Mottashed Marselle Harrison-Miles

Tahiri Varner Teresa Rice Natasha Naderi

Rosalind Swainson Langston Story

Karyta Byers Eloise Hudgins

Ramona Bryant Marlon Knight Mercy Varner

Jurrell Howell, Sr. Mary Ann Varner

Candice Nash Hooker Jayto Somah-Cassell

Adzoa Brown Kimberly Brown Kevin Chuck Brown

Alexis Champion Daphne McNabb Shamika Shahid Ebony Glass

Laura Bucci Masovaida Morgan Brian Burrell Lestra Bradham

Nicole Kelly Tahiri Hudson Sherry Chatham Mary Gary Cooper

Robin Turner TaQuila Thomas Morgan Tinsley Myles Tinsley

Darmeshia West Shannon Jetter Farris Johnson Ruth M. Oyola

Princess Ramos Keith L. Brown Zamani Williams Noelani Adan

Table of Contents

Prelude of Sound

shhh...listen.
This book is alive with music.
Each chapter carries a song.
Press play and let the words and melodies
Glow together in your hands.

You will find the playlist here:
www.myjoyglows.com/books

INTRODUCTION

The Parable of the Chameleon and the Butterfly

As told by the wings that rose, not the shadow that fled.

Once upon a hush before healing, in a sun-drenched forest woven of illusion and light, there lived a Chameleon named Croix and Butterfly named Solana. Croix was captivating. He spoke in smooth tones and soft glances. He mirrored your dreams back to you, until you couldn't tell where his reflection ended and your truth began. He made you feel chosen, then questioned. Seen, then silenced. Loved, until you forgot what love really felt like.

And Solana? She didn't have to try to shine. She simply did. She laughed in colors, danced with the breeze, and believed, perhaps too deeply, in the goodness of souls. When Croix said, "I see you," she stayed.

Because like so many of us, she was hungry to be welcomed, loved, and cared for. But admiration has a short shelf life in the eyes of someone who envies your light.

Croix loved her wings, until he realized they could carry her places he could never go. So he did what insecure hearts do:
He clipped, questioned, shadowed,
and called it love.

At first, she bent.
She twisted herself into his shade just to feel safe.
Just to stay "seen."
But shrinking doesn't equal safety.
And love that asks you to disappear isn't love,
it's possession.

One day, in the quiet ache between who she'd become and who she used to be, Solana realized:
Her wings hadn't withered.
They were waiting.

Waiting for her to remember they were never meant to be hidden, they were meant to fly.
So, she left.

Not with rage.

But with remembrance.

She rose from the branch that never held her.

And in her rising, she finally understood:

Croix didn't love her.

He loved control.

And love without freedom is just a prettier name for fear.

She didn't seek revenge.

She sought resurrection.

And bloom by bloom,

feather by flame,

she became louder, softer, wiser, wilder.

If you asked her today what she thinks of the Chameleon,

she'd smile gently and say:

"He taught me how to spot manipulation…

and how never to confuse it with magic."

Dear Reader...

You are Solana. You've survived the shapeshifters.
You've bent to fit into places you've outgrown.
You've questioned your light because someone else
couldn't hold it.

But this book isn't about them. It's about you.
It's about reclaiming your wings. Unlearning the lies
that told you to shrink. Healing the parts of you
that forgot:
You were never meant to blend in. You were born to
glow through it all.

This is a fable soaked in truth.
Dressed in beauty.
Sharper than it seems.

Let the rising begin!

-Volari

CHAPTER
01

The Chameleon Season

Croix & Solana

The Chameleon Moves In

A fable with Sass, Soul, and a Moral

roix the Chameleon had colors for every occasion, Church? He was holy. A date? He was soulful. Family BBQ? He could grill lies medium rare. And then came Solana, the Butterfly with laugh lines around her eyes and boundaries made of glitter and steel.

"Why do you always have to match the scenery?" she asked one day, watching Croix slide into a new crowd with a brand-new accent.

"I'm just adaptable, baby," Croix said, flashing a grin that had broken hearts in seven zip codes

"Adaptable or unstable?" Solana raised an eyebrow. "Because you change so much, I'm getting emotional whiplash."

Croix blinked slowly. "I become what people need me to be."

"That's not noble," she said, as her wings twitched. "That's exhausting."

But Solana stayed. At first.

Until she realized that Croix didn't just blend into his surroundings,

He erased hers.

Moral
Just because someone fits in everywhere… Doesn't mean they fit nor belong with you.

Q&A for the Soul

- Have you ever met someone who was "everything you needed" ...until they weren't?

_____

_____

_____

_____

_____

- What masks have you worn to feel safe?

_____

_____

_____

_____

_____

- How did you finally shed them?

_____

_____

_____

_____

_____

The Mirror Lie

I morphed into someone new, and my soul felt completely vacuumed of air. I didn't feel like my old self or this person looking at me in the mirror. I wondered if others would take me seriously. Respected, loved, and treated me the way I deserved, even behind my mask, lighting up just enough to be seen for who I really was. It depended on the day and who I was standing in front of. I had become a master shapeshifter.

Like a chameleon in a house of mirrors,

I adjusted to every glare and expectation.

In relationships, I mirrored their moods.

At work, I became what the job needed.

In friendships, I shrank so others could shine.

But the more I adapted, the more invisible I became.

One day, I caught a glimpse of myself in a window.

Hair pulled tight. Smile tight. Eyes...tired.

I didn't recognize her.

It was the first time I realized: I was building my whole identity on reflections that weren't mine.

And the mirror?

It lied.

She Used to Be Silent

She used to be silent.
Used to flinch when they raised their voice,
Or raised their glass.
Or raised the stakes.
She used to say, "it's okay"
When it wasn't.
Smile
When she wanted to scream.
Forgive
What she never deserved.
She wore diplomacy like armor.
Wore her trauma like perfume,
Invisible, but always in the room.
But one day…
She stopped shrinking.
She started singing in her shower again.
She said no with her whole chest.
She laughed too loud on purpose.
She became a woman who didn't wait to be chosen,
She chose herself.

Truth Nugget

A Soul Breakdown from the Garden of Croix & Solana

> *Just because someone fits in everywhere... doesn't mean they fit nor belong with you."*
> *– Narrated Wisdom, The Chameleon Season*

Here's What It Means:

This line slices through the illusion of charm.

People like Croix can morph into anyone to feel accepted, they adapt, flatter, and mirror what others need. But being adaptable isn't the same as being authentic. Fitting in doesn't guarantee alignment, trust, or truth.

This quote is a warning wrapped in poetry.

It's the difference between chemistry and compatibility, between presence and partnership. Someone might slide easily into every room, every role, every version of love, but if they disappear when things get real, that's not love. That's performance.

Why the Character Says It:

This line is narrated, not spoken by Solana or Croix directly, because it's a universal truth. It comes from the voice of experience, the narrator who has lived through this pattern enough to name it.

Solana doesn't need to say this out loud, she lives it.

She stays long enough to see it, feel it, and eventually leave it. That line is the echo of her wisdom after she flies away.

Did You Know?

The Chameleon Illusion

Chameleons don't actually change colors to match their environment. They change based on mood, temperature, and light. Chameleons don't change colors to hide. They shift hues to regulate temperature and communicate emotions, like stress, fear, and attraction.

Their "color-matching" reputation? A myth.

Just like people who claim to "just be whatever you need."

Let this remind you:

Real connection isn't about blending in;

It's about showing up real.

Translation for Life:

In real life, we often confuse someone's versatility with depth. We romanticize the "social chameleon", the one who makes everyone feel special. But that's not always a gift. Sometimes, it's a mask.

Here's what this quote teaches us:

Watch who disappears when your needs show up.

Beware of those who blend in effortlessly, because they often stand for nothing.

Don't confuse charisma with character.

Let this line give you permission to raise your standards, trust your intuition, and believe that belonging is not about convenience, it's about truth.

Healing Reflection

Ask yourself:

- ➢ Where in my life have, I learned to blend in just to survive?
- ➢ What part of me has been performing safely, while secretly craving freedom?
- ➢ Who did I have to become to feel lovable, and is that person still running the show?
- ➢ What would it feel like to choose visibility over approval?

Croix reminds us:

You can master the art of disappearing and still feel unseen.

Solana reminds us:

Just because they applauded your performance doesn't mean they ever knew your soul.

And you, dear one,

You don't owe anyone the version of you that kept the peace at the expense of your truth.

Healing begins when you stop asking, "Will they still love me if I change?"

And start declaring, "I love me enough to stop changing for them."

Empowerment & Self-Compassion Challenge

Affirmations

- ➢ I no longer shrink myself to keep shapeshifters comfortable.
- ➢ I deserve to feel seen without sacrificing my soul.
- ➢ I do not have to shrink to be safe.
- ➢ I was not made to match the walls.
- ➢ My voice belongs in every room I enter.
- ➢ I honor the truth of who I am, not who they want me to be.

Journaling Prompts

- Who taught you it was safer to blend in than to stand out?

_____

_____

_____

_____

_____

- Write about a time you adapted to survive. What did it cost you?

_____

_____

_____

_____

_____

- What does your true voice sound like when no one's watching?

_____

_____

_____

_____

_____

Self-Compassion Challenge

Light a candle.

Stand in front of a mirror.

Say your name out loud, slowly, clearly.

Then say:

"This is who I am when no one else is looking. And I am enough."

CHAPTER
02

Shapeshifter

Croix & Solana

The Chrysalis Chronicles Continue

"The Shape-Shift Soiree"

*I*t was a velvety moonlit night at the Gathering of Great Thinkers, a mystical salon held once a month under a canopy of glowing leaves and humming truth-flowers. The air buzzed with the scent of revelation and rosehips. A crystalline tree shimmered at the center, glowing like the truth no one wanted to say out loud.

Croix the Chameleon arrived draped in his usual disguise, his signature pinstripe suit that changed hues every time the conversation got deep. It was the one that shifted colors every time the conversation turned real. It shimmered emerald when he lied, charcoal when he deflected, and a brief flicker of indigo when he almost told the truth.

Solana, radiant as ever, had just entered the Gathering of Great Thinkers, for the monthly moonlit meet-up of magical beings. She was luminous and grounded, floated in wearing wings that caught the moonlight like stained glass. She wasn't here for surface talk.

"Darlin', you look like a moonbeam drippin' in lavender," Croix purred. "But I must ask, did you come to inspire or interrogate?"

Solana tilted her head, voice light as honey but sharp as crystal. "Depends," Solana quipped, fanning her wings. "Are you shapeshifting to protect your heart or to dodge accountability?"

Croix leaned back, sipped from his tea, and muttered,
"You ever look in the mirror and not even recognize who's lookin' back? You start wonderin' if that reflection paid rent to live in your face?"

Solana deadpanned, "Every Monday after a full weekend of pretending to be 'low-maintenance." From behind a crystalline tree, a sparkle shot into the clearing, it was Just then, whoosh! A sequin-storm blew through the clearing.

Enter Zephyr Blaze, the fire-breathing fairy who only wore sequins, platform boots and truth like a badge.
"Ahem! Time for truths and tea!" he bellowed. "Shape-shifting isn't self-care, baby," he cackled. "That's identity theft with good intentions! Let the shapeshifters sip and the butterflies bloom!"

From the shadows emerged Bella Boom, all hips swaying and holy hell, strutting like the world owed her backpay in joy, wearing six-inch heels echoing like declarations and lashes longer than most relationships. The bodacious butterfly brawler dropped her voice low enough to crack a soul open.

"Girl, you can't please everybody. This isn't a buffet. Stop servin' pieces of yourself on every single plate."

Then she whispered,

"You're not soft for shapeshifting, Solana," she said with a snap.

"You're sacred for surviving. But girl, surviving isn't the same as living."

Sir Katticus Flame, dignified and low-key spicy, lifted a chalice of cosmic cocoa.

"Y'all ever notice how chameleons get really nervous when the lighting gets real?" he mused.

"Truth got a way of turning camo into clear coats."

Then a swirl of glitter rained down. It wasn't magic, it was Nixie Starfire, half-stardust, half-side-eye, floating in on a breeze of glitter and grit.

"You weren't born to camouflage in chaos," she whispered to Solana.

"You were born to shine so hard the darkness has to squint."

Croix chuckled uneasily. Solana didn't flinch.

The lights dimmed, the spotlight found her.

Croix blinked.

Solana raised one brow and smiled in amusement. The spotlight was on.

Croix blinked again.

There was Sir Katticus Flame, still sipping from his chalice of cosmic cocoa. A golden purr interrupted the moment, this feline philosopher and moonshine connoisseur, spoke from his velvet perch,

"Even a chameleon gets tired of changing colors. But the butterfly? She paints the sky and calls it freedom."

Nixie Starfire twirled mid-air and pointed at Solana like she was giving her the final key.

"You were born to sparkle," Nixie declared, "not to camouflage in dysfunction!"

Everyone paused.

Croix opened his mouth to speak, but the mirror between them started to glow, not with illusion, but clarity.

Solana smiled.

"Now that's what I call a reflection."

Moral

Adapting is not a flaw. Adapting is survival. But when your identity bends so much it forgets itself, and you disappear, it's time to molt. You were never meant to be a mirrorball for other people's insecurities.

Q&A for the Soul

- Who am I when no one is watching?

_____

_____

_____

_____

_____

- Do I shrink to survive, or do I stretch to be seen?

_____

_____

_____

_____

_____

- Am I changing to stay safe… or am I betraying myself to stay liked?

_____

_____

_____

_____

_____

- What would happen if I stopped apologizing for needing space?

_____

_____

_____

_____

_____

Becoming What They Needed

I once received a glowing review that called me "easy to work
with, flexible."
I smiled and nodded.
But inside?
I was folding.
They praised my adaptability,
not realizing it was a mask I wore,
so no one would ask too many questions,
so no one would see me crack.
I could shift my tone mid-sentence
depending on who entered the room.
A mood reader.
A shapeshifter.
A peacekeeper in pearls.
I adjusted my light to soothe others,
dimmed my truth to avoid conflict,
and wore my silence like armor wrapped in a smile.
Once, I even changed my laugh,
shrunk it into something soft and palatable
after someone said it was "too much."
And when I looked in the mirror...
I couldn't find the sound anymore.

There was a time Solana thought her gift was adaptability.

She was the girlfriend who never "nagged,"

the daughter who never "talked back,"

the employee who smiled through twelve-hour days.

She bent so far for others,

her spine forgot how to stand.

They called her "easy to love,"

but what they really meant was:

"You're convenient."

In every room, she read the temperature,

measured her words,

offered comfort at her own expense.

She laughed at jokes that crossed her boundaries,

clapped for people who had dimmed her light.

It wasn't performance, it was survival.

Until one night, bathed in the silence of her bathroom mirror,

with mascara smudged and courage whispering,

she exhaled the truth:

"I miss me."

Survival Style

I wore my silence like silk,
My smile like war paint,
My walk rehearsed,
My voice shrink-wrapped.
Not because I lacked truth,
But because I feared it.
And when fear becomes fashion,
It frays the seams of your soul.

Truth Nugget

> *"Girl, you can't please everybody. This isn't a buffet. Stop servin' pieces of yourself on every single plate."*
> *– Bella Boom*

Here's What It Means:

This quote is a raw reminder that trying to keep everyone happy will leave you empty. It's not noble, it's self-neglect. When you keep slicing off parts of yourself to serve others, eventually there's nothing left for you.

Bella's line slices through the polite lies we tell ourselves:

That being agreeable is the same as being kind.

That sacrificing your needs is how you earn love.

Spoiler: It's not.

Why the Character Says It:

Bella Boom doesn't do masks, mirrors, or maybes. She says what Solana is too exhausted to admit: that she's been performing emotional CPR on people who never brought breath of their own.

Bella sees Solana's people-pleasing as a trauma reflex, not a personality trait.

She's not scolding Solana, she's calling her home to herself.

Did You Know?

Chameleons molt; often and quietly. Unlike snakes, who shed all at once, chameleons release their old skin in pieces, over time. It's not always pretty. It's not always noticed. But it's necessary. Molting isn't a flaw. It's a function of growth. When the inner self expands, the old skin must go. Even if it flakes. Even if it lingers.

Just like us, chameleons don't need applause to evolve. Their transformation happens in private, bit by bit, until they're renewed.

You don't have to rush your shedding. You just have to honor the pieces falling away.

Translation for Life:

You are not a buffet. You are not a vending machine. You are not a spiritual pantry for the emotionally underfed.
The people who expect you to keep giving without ever asking how you're holding up? They're not your people.

This quote gives permission to draw a line and say:
"I'm not offering myself in pieces anymore. I'm not sacrificing my peace to keep the party going."

Did You Know?

Butterflies shed, too, but not like you think. Before they ever fly, they molt five times as caterpillars. Each time, they grow out of their skin. Each time, they get closer to their wings. And the final transformation? It happens in the dark. Inside the chrysalis, the caterpillar doesn't just grow wings, it dissolves into almost nothing and rebuilds from within. Metamorphosis is messy magic. But that goo becomes glory.

So, if you're breaking down, breaking open, or breaking free...
You're not failing. You're forming.

Real connection isn't *about blending in,*
It's about showing up real.

Healing Reflection

Ask yourself:

➢ Where have I been over-serving?

➢ Who am I still trying to prove my worth to, and why?

➢ What would it look like to stop over-delivering and start receiving?

➢ Who benefits when I shrink?

➢ When did I learn that my worth was measured by how easy I was to love?

➢ What would it feel like to be whole in a world that keeps asking for pieces?

If this quote stung a little… good. That sting is honesty waking you up. Because the next time someone comes with an empty plate expecting your joy, energy, time, or softness, you'll smile, shake your head gently, and say:

"I'm not on the menu anymore."

There's a grief that comes with people-pleasing, the quiet ache of being everything to everyone except yourself.

You become fluent in reading the room but forget how to listen to your own heartbeat.

You laugh softer, speak less, and contort yourself into palatable shapes, hoping someone will finally call you enough.

But as Bella Boom reminds us, this is not a buffet. Your soul was never meant to be picked apart like side dishes.

You are the full meal. Sacred. Nourishing. Whole.
And anyone who doesn't honor that wholeness? Doesn't deserve a seat at your table.

Healing whispers:

You don't need to earn love through exhaustion.
You are worthy of rest, of softness, of saying "no" without explanation.
You were never meant to perform your way into belonging.
You were meant to belong to yourself.

Empowerment & Self-Compassion Challenge
Unmasking

Affirmation

> ➤ I am not required to morph into comfort for others.
> ➤ My truth deserves space.

Journaling Prompts:

- In what spaces do I feel I have to shift to be accepted?

_____

_____

_____

_____

_____

- Who am I afraid to disappoint by being my full self?

_____

_____

_____

_____

_____

- What part of me am I ready to reintroduce to the world?

_____

_____

_____

_____

_____

Self-Compassion Challenge

Write a letter from your "unmasked" self to your present self. Let it be raw. Let it be kind.

CHAPTER

03

The Mirror Lied

Croix & Solana

The Glass House Gasp

A Parable of Distorted Reflections and Cracking Truths

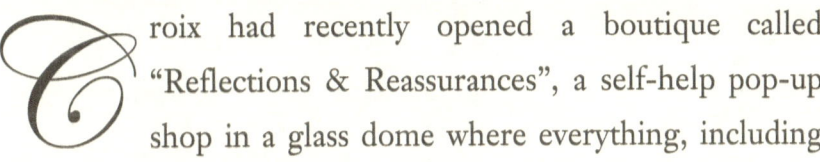

Croix had recently opened a boutique called "Reflections & Reassurances", a self-help pop-up shop in a glass dome where everything, including the truth, came with a filter.

Inside, the mirrors were rigged. Not the kind that told you, you were the fairest, but the kind that told you what you wanted to hear, especially if you were insecure.

Solana fluttered in, her wings twitching with curiosity.
"Welcome, beloved," Croix said, voice dripping with false calm. "Here, you can see yourself through the eyes of those who adore you. No truth, no trauma, just tailored delusion."

Solana raised a brow. "So basically, lies on layaway?"

From the corner, Zephyr Blaze cartwheeled in wearing a disco-ball jumpsuit.

"Croix, you out here selling curated gaslighting like it's aromatherapy," he gasped. "Sir, this isn't healing, it's hallucinating!"

Bella Boom, sipping lemon balm tea with red lipstick like war paint, kicked off her heel and hollered, "Some folks don't want clarity, they want comfort that comes with compliments!"

Sir Katticus Flame emerged from the shadows with a magnifying glass. "These aren't mirrors," he said. "These are funhouse deceptions. There's nothing fun about losing your whole self in the mirror maze and losing yourself in your own reflection."

Cue Nixie Starfire, floating above them like a constellation with attitude. "This whole dome," she snapped, "is just a trick to keep you from trusting your own reflection. Smash it, Solana."

And just like that, Solana looked into one final mirror, saw her dimmed light, the smudges of compromise, and the cracks in her confidence. Then she exhaled.

One wing swiped across the glass. Shatter.

Moral

If someone keeps warping your reflection to control how you see yourself, it's time to leave the mirror and the room.

Q&A for the Soul

- Have you ever doubted your truth because someone insisted you were wrong?

_____

_____

_____

_____

_____

- How do you tell the difference between feedback and manipulation?

_____

_____

_____

_____

_____

- What does your soul know that your fear tries to silence?

_____

_____

_____

_____

_____

Through Their Eyes, I Disappeared

They didn't hit me. Not with hands.

The hit was with phrases like:

"You're too sensitive."

"You always make things bigger than they are."

"That never happened."

I started keeping receipts. Screenshots. Voicemails. Because I needed proof of my reality.

I wasn't "crazy", I was being gaslit.

They could charm a room and silence my voice with a smirk. I used to practice what I wanted to say out loud, but when the moment came, I froze. Or worse, laughed it off.

I became the queen of over-explaining, apologizing for my tone before I even spoke.

There were nights I would replay conversations in my head like a courtroom transcript, trying to prove I wasn't broken.

But I wasn't broken.

I was being broken into.

Emotionally, spiritually, energetically. Until I wasn't sure what was mine anymore.

Until one day, I woke up in a room full of people and still felt invisible.

I knew then:

I had made myself small enough to fit in his version of reality.
And now it was time to leave.

The Mirror Lied

They held up a mirror
and called it love,
But it was warped glass
and dim light.
It told me I was too much,
too loud,
too emotional,
too intense.
Too real.
So, I edited myself.
Trimmed the parts that shined.
Muted the colors that sang.
Softened the truths that burned.
Until I couldn't find the reflection I once knew,
Only a quiet girl with eyes
that stopped asking to be seen.
But now I know:
The mirror lied.
And I won't live inside a lie.

Truth Nugget

> *"If he wanted to be part of your healing, baby, he wouldn't have been the wound."*
> *– Nixie Starfire*

Here's What It Means:

Not everyone who returns deserves a reentry.
Not every apology is a passport.
Nixie's line is a glittery, gut-punch of truth: If someone chooses to harm you, they forfeit the privilege of guiding your recovery.

This quote calls out the seduction of nostalgia and false redemption. We want to believe people change. But sometimes the one who caused the most damage, the one who caused the deepest scar comes back, with soft words and rehearsed regret, wearing remorse like perfume, and hoping we forgot the fire they started, the same and exact fire they lit.

Why the Character Says It:

Nixie is sparkle and steel.
She's the friend who won't let you fall for the rerun of your own heartbreak.

When she says this to Solana, it's not just shade, it's sacred intervention. It's soul defense.

But Nixie knows, those who crack your wings don't get front-row seats to admire your healing glow. She sees Croix returning, cloaked in remorse and charm, trying to re-enter through the soft door of Solana's forgiveness.

Did You Know?

Gaslighting is a form of psychological manipulation where someone causes you to doubt your own memory, perception, or sanity. It's often subtle and that's what makes it so dangerous.

Butterflies rely on pattern memory. If a predator hurt them in their caterpillar stage, they retain the memory and avoid that scent in adulthood.

Let this be your permission:

You don't owe second chances to what already tried to erase you.

Translation for Life:

This quote is for:

The woman who replies to a text from the same number that once left her crying in her car.

The man who replays an apology from the person who shattered his self-worth, like it's a promise, when it's just a loop of old manipulation.

It's for you and anyone who has ever confused a familiar voice with a safe one.

Nixie reminds us:

If they broke you, they can't build you.

If they couldn't honor and respect you when they had access, they don't get VIP passes when you rise.

Your healing isn't a sequel they're entitled to watch.

You owe no encore to the ones who missed your worth the first time.

Healing Reflection

Ask yourself:

> ➢ Am I mistaking regret for change?
> ➢ Am I longing for closure or craving connection?
> ➢ Would I let this person near my glow if I didn't have history with them?

Healing Whispers:

Healing is not a group project.

Especially not with the person who handed you the hammer and watched you break doesn't get to help you rebuild your wings.

Let this quote be your lighthouse and boundary wrapped in beauty:

You are allowed to rise without reaching back.

You are allowed to glow, brighter, bolder, freer, without letting them or making room to give them another chance to dim you... again.

Empowerment & Self-Compassion Challenge

Affirmations:

> ➤ My truth is valid, even when others try to rewrite it.
> ➤ I no longer question my reality to make others comfortable.
> ➤ I trust my intuition. I believe in myself.

Journaling Prompts:

- When was the last time someone made you question your truth?

_____

_____

_____

_____

_____

- What patterns of gaslighting have you experienced or witnessed?

_____

_____

_____

_____

_____

_____

_____

_____

_____

_____

- How can you begin reclaiming your voice today?

_____

_____

_____

_____

_____

_____

_____

_____

_____

Self-Compassion Challenge

Write a letter to your reflection.

Apologize for doubting yourself.

Thank yourself for surviving.

Promise yourself you'll never be silenced again.

CHAPTER

04

When the Colors Faded

Croix & Solana

The Bleaching of Bright Things

A Chrysalis Chronicle Parable

Scene: The Celestial Conservatory sanctuary where colors hum, vibes glow, and emotions paint the air like smoke signals from the soul.

*S*olana perched on a quartz bench beneath a glowing vine canopy. Her wings, once bursting with teal, plum, and gold, now looked faint, like they'd been washed one too many times in someone else's storm.

Croix sauntered in wearing his "I'm just misunderstood" hue, a dull gray-blue that matched his mood and excuses.
"Darlin', you look… different," he said, trying to sound concerned but coming off condescending.

"I feel different," Solana replied softly, brushing dust off her once radiant wings.

Zephyr Blaze flounced into the conservatory, glitter trailing behind like emotional support confetti.
"Y'all see this nonsense?" he huffed, pointing at Croix's color. "He's out here serving Eeyore energy, draining the room with that moody pastel!"

Bella Boom clacked in, heels slicing silence like declarations. "You don't owe anyone your light, Solana. Especially not someone who dims it on purpose."

Sir Katticus Flame stepped from the shadows, monocle gleaming. "Even a candle gets tired of burning at both ends. Take care before your flame forgets it's fire."

Nixie Starfire spiraled overhead, leaving stardust and tough love in her wake. "Glow fatigue is real. Stop being the power source for someone else's drama lamp."

Croix blinked. Solana blinked back, slower, steadier. Not out of fear, but resolve.

She stood, stretched her wings, and said,
"If you can't hold space for my color, you don't deserve my light."

Moral

Know your worth, and guard it with care,
Set boundaries firm, like a breath of fresh air.

Q&A for the Soul:

- What parts of me have dimmed in the name of peace?

_____

_____

_____

_____

_____

- Who drains my light, and who helps me refill it?

_____

_____

_____

_____

_____

- What would rest look like if it felt like a birthright, not a reward?

_____

_____

_____

_____

_____

The Glow That Got Gutted

There was a time I didn't feel tired. I felt erased.

I wasn't just burnt out, I was burnt through.

They said I was "the strong one," the "reliable one," the "light in the room."

But no one ever asked what it cost to shine like that, every single day.

Nobody asked about the price tag of that glow.

No one stopped to wonder what it took to shine like that day after day.

For me or any others.

Nobody questioned the weight she carried just to stay that bright.

No one ever asked what she had to burn through just to glow like that.

Nobody asked what it drained from her to stay that radiant every day.

I was overextending myself in conversations, in care, in keeping peace.

Smiling while suppressing. Laughing while leaking.

Even joy felt like labor.

I remember sitting at dinner with friends, nodding along, sipping water like it was wine,

while my soul screamed, "I don't want to be here."

That was my breaking point, not with rage, but with silence.
I didn't explode. I evaporated.
And in that disappearance, I met the version of me that I had been abandoning all along.

Her Bright Began to Fade

She didn't burn out like fire,
She faded like a sky once kissed by sunset,
Now pale with other people's shadows.
Her yes became habitual.
Her no became a whisper.
Her light, a memory.
She didn't lose herself.
She gave herself away piece by piece,
Until she forgot how whole felt.
But even dusk holds the promise of dawn.
And she?
She's setting boundaries like stars now.

Truth Nugget

> *"He didn't love you in the dark. He just liked that you couldn't see the cracks."*
> *– Zephyr Blaze*

Here's What It Means:

This quote slices through illusion like moonlight on shattered glass.

It reveals a painful truth: Some people don't love you, they love your blindness.

He didn't celebrate your vulnerability, he exploited it.

He didn't cover you in light, he dimmed the room to mask his own shadows.

The darkness wasn't intimacy. It was camouflage.

Why the Character Says It:

Zephyr Blaze, ever flamboyant and fiercely wise, delivers this line while examining the emotional architecture of a toxic relationship. In Chapter 4, Solana begins to realize that her so-called "safe space" was never lit with love, it was just dimmed to keep her docile.

Zephyr sees it for what it is: a power play disguised as passion.

With his usual sparkle and sting, he names the manipulation. It's not romantic. It's a trap wrapped in velvet.

> ## Did You Know?
>
> Some butterflies lose wing pigment when stressed or overexposed to pollution, just like we lose our shine when we stay in toxic environments too long. Chameleons can stop changing colors when they're sick, depressed, or dying. Translation? Color tells the truth even when the mouth stays silent.

Translation for Life:

Have you ever felt "close" to someone, but you couldn't quite breathe?

Have you mistaken silence for peace?

Stillness for safety?

Sometimes what we call "comfort" is just the absence of visibility. And the person who benefits from your confusion... never had your clarity in mind.

This quote is for every survivor who walked away from a love that only felt good in low light.

For every person who looked back and realized:

It wasn't deep, it was dark.

Healing Reflection:

Ask yourself:

- ➤ Who flourished when I was small?
- ➤ What "romantic" memories lose their glow when I turn the lights all the way on?
- ➤ Do I confuse quietness with kindness?

Zephyr reminds us:

- ➤ You deserve to be loved with the lights on.
- ➤ Flaws visible. Hearts honest.
- ➤ No shadows. No guessing games. No distortion.

Healing Whispers

If they couldn't cherish your brilliance in full light, they were never worthy of standing in your sun.

Empowerment & Self-Compassion Challenge

Insight

You are not the fixer, the emotional sponge, or the team mascot for grown people with unhealed wounds. Your energy is sacred.

Affirmations:

➢ My light is not up for negotiation.

➢ I choose peace over performance.

➢ Rest is revolutionary. And I deserve it.

Journaling Prompts:

• Where am I giving from depletion, not overflow?

_____

_____

_____

_____

_____

• Who do I feel I "owe" energy to, and why?

_____

_____

_____

_____

_____

- What would reclaiming my light look like in small daily ways?

_____

_____

_____

_____

_____

Self-Compassion Challenge

Create a "Glow List":

Write down five activities, people, or places that refill your spirit.

1. _____

2. _____

3. _____

4. _____

5. _____

Then schedule one each week like a non-negotiable appointment with your joy.

You have to be intentional since Joy is not a luxury, it's a necessity for a thriving, soulful life.

Here are a few ideas to inspire you:

> ➢ Coffee or tea with a soul-filling friend
> ➢ A slow walk in your favorite park
> ➢ An afternoon with a book that makes your heart light
> ➢ A creative session, painting, writing, making music, or even pottery (Ask me about it, I have a friend and sister, Sarah, who teaches classes)

> ➤ Quiet time with your thoughts, prayers, or meditation (I can help you with this or even host a sound bathing experience for you and your friends).

Let this be your weekly reminder that you matter, your joy matters, and your glow is worth prioritizing.

Weekly Joy Planner Example

DAY OF JOY	PLANS / NOTES	DATE
MONDAY		
TUESDAY		
WEDNESDAY		
THURSDAY		
FRIDAY		
SATURDAY		
SUNDAY		

CHAPTER
05

Shedding Skins

Croix & Solana

The Chrysalis Chronicles Continue
"The Great Shedding Soirée"

A comic-soul fable with glitter and gumption

*I*t was transformation season at the Gathering of Great Thinkers, a time when magical beings shed what no longer served them. The air buzzed with release. Old habits were hung like coats. Masks melted like mist. Even the moon looked like it was letting go of its shadows.

Croix the Chameleon showed up in snakeskin boots and a faux-spiritual poncho, preaching about "evolution" like he invented the concept.

"I've been reborn," he said, tossing incense into the fire with flair. "I'm not that same chameleon anymore."
Solana arched a wing and smirked. "You sure? Or did you just rebrand your avoidance and call it healing?"

From the canopy above, Zephyr Blaze flipped down with glitter raining from his wings and twirled into the firelight like a disco ball dipped in truth. "Ooooh, she scalpel-snatched your whole enlightenment arc, babe!"

"You ever notice how exes text right when your therapist says, 'don't reach out'?" he said, twinkling with just enough sarcasm to exfoliate a soul.

"Let's be real, sugar, if healing had a face, half y'all would swipe left. Croix is not the one either. He doesn't reply fast, and he deletes your ex's number before you even blink!"

Croix blinked. Then blinked again. Like his internal Wi-Fi just cut out.

Solana didn't even turn her head. Growth had her full attention.

Zephyr Blaze then swirled through the smoke like a disco phoenix.

Bella Boom stomped in, snatching off a wig labeled "Perfection."
"If it doesn't fit anymore, baby, it goes in the fire."

Sir Katticus Flame stirred a pot of ancestral tea and declared, "Real growth doesn't come with hashtags, it comes with challenges You gotta cry for the versions of you that kept you safe, even if they no longer serve you."

Nixie Starfire hovered near Solana, handing her a tiny, radiant knife. "It's time," she whispered. "Cut the cord. But do it with compassion. That girl you used to be? She survived so you could thrive."

Croix, unsure whether to hug or run, glanced at Solana. "So… you just gonna let all that go?"

She exhaled. "No. I'm going to honor it. Then release it." The flames crackled. Old selves turned to stardust. Solana glowed, not because she was new, but because she was whole.

Moral
You don't heal by hating who you were. You heal by thanking yourself for getting you this far… and stepping boldly into your next chapter.

Q&A for the Soul

- What beliefs or behaviors are you outgrowing?

_____

_____

_____

_____

_____

- What parts of your old self deserve a proper goodbye?

_____

_____

_____

_____

_____

- What would happen if you honored your healing instead of rushing it?

_____

_____

_____

_____

_____

Grief in the Growth

There's a secret they don't tell you about healing:

You don't just lose the pain.

You lose the version of you who carried it.

There was a version of me who carried the world in her smile and broke in silence.

She held it together with to-do lists and soft apologies.

She cheered for others while burying her own exhaustion.

People called her strong. Reliable. The go-to.

But no one ever asked what it cost to shine like that every single day.

I had a version of me who was always "the strong one."

She held the tears in her throat, the rage in her gut, and the dreams in her back pocket.

She smiled through betrayal. Laughed through panic.

She was the fire that stayed lit throughout the storm.

Because she was a force of nature.

An earthquake in heels.

And even in her weakest moments,

someone others would whisper about, not for how loud she fought...

but for how long she carried things no one else could see.

And she was tired.

When I started healing, I missed her.

I missed the girl who always had a plan. Who could pivot through a storm like she was dancing.

But I had to let her go.

She got me here...

But she couldn't take me where I was going.

So, I wept.

Not for the pain, but for the girl who survived it.

I lit a candle, whispered her name, and said thank you.

Then I chose softness over armor.

Peace over performance.

Me... over survival.

And when I finally laid her to rest, the girl who never asked for help, I didn't just grieve her.

I honored her.

And now?

I rise not in spite of her, but because of her.

She survived so I could be free.

When I Said Goodbye

I didn't rage.
I didn't scream.
I didn't write a monologue for the pain.
I made tea.
I sat in silence with the girl I used to be,
Held her hand,
Listened to her story,
And said,
"I forgive you for staying too long.
I honor you for holding it all.
But you don't have to protect me anymore.
I've got it now."
And when she exhaled,
The whole sky shifted.

Truth Nugget

> *"You ever notice how exes text right when your therapist says, 'don't reach out'?"*
> *– Zephyr Blaze*

Here's What It Means:

Timing isn't always a coincidence, it's often resistance in disguise.

Just when you start to feel whole again…

Just when your therapist finally gets you to delete the thread and block the number…

Right when you're finally getting clear, reclaiming your worth, and choosing peace over patterns,

Boom. A "Hey stranger" appears, like clockwork and chaos rolled into one.

Old temptations come disguised as "maybe this time will be different."

Old patterns don't like being evicted.

And sometimes, the past comes knocking dressed in déjà vu, hoping you'll mistake it for destiny.

Spoiler alert: It usually isn't.

> ## *Did You Know?*
>
> Butterflies must struggle to break free from their chrysalis.
>
> If you help them, they won't survive, because the pressure is what strengthens their wings.
>
> Butterflies don't have vocal cords, but they communicate through wing patterns and vibrations. Like them, your essence can express itself in countless ways.
>
> Studies show that speaking your truth activates areas of the brain associated with courage, confidence, and healing. Your voice isn't just sound, it's self-ownership in motion.

Why The Character Says It:

Zephyr Blaze is the glitter-slicked truth-teller of the soul crew.

He knows healing isn't a straight line, it zigzags, doubles back, and sometimes gets lost in old playlists and photo memories, then it has loops, flashbacks, and shady pop quizzes.

This line?

It's not just sass. It's spiritual comic relief.

He's throwing glittery warning signs around the trapdoors in your growth journey, especially the ones that look like "maybe they've changed."

This line is his sparkly reminder that distractions often show up dressed as nostalgia. He's not just being funny, he's throwing a flare across the emotional minefield of "should I respond?"

Because he knows: the biggest glow-down comes from mistaking interruption for intention.

Translation for Life:

This is for anyone who's mid-glow-up and gets that "WYD?" text from someone who didn't know what to do with your heart the first time.

Zephyr reminds us:

You don't owe your past a response.

You don't need to explain your silence.

Growth is when peace shows up…and you finally answer that call instead.

You're allowed to block the number, protect your progress, and choose your future over recycled feelings.

When the past shows up during your healing season, pause. Breathe. Don't let your progress get hijacked by a text that sounds sweet but smells like déjà vu. Growth means you don't have to answer every knock; especially when peace is finally at your door.

Did You Know?

Chameleons shed their skin regularly to grow.

If they resist the process, their health suffers.

Shedding isn't failure it's life doing its sacred work.

You, dear reader, are not broken.

You are in the shedding.

And you're doing it beautifully.

Healing Reflection

Ask yourself:

> ➤ Am I craving them, or just craving the comfort of not starting over?
> ➤ Do I miss them, or do I miss who I hoped they would be?
> ➤ Am I healing… or holding space for a ghost?

Healing Whispers

You deserve a glow-up that's sacred, not sabotaged.

Every time you say no to what broke you, you say yes to what can bless you.

Let this be your reminder:

You are not a rehab center for the emotionally unavailable.

You are the sanctuary now.

And your peace? Non-refundable.

Empowerment & Self-Compassion Challenge The Release

Affirmations

> ➤ I thank my past self for her strength.
>
> ➤ I honor what I had to do to survive.
>
> ➤ I release shame. I choose grace.
>
> ➤ I am no longer who I was… and that is holy.

Journaling Prompts

• Who was I pretending to be, just to be loved? What part of me did I change to accommodate someone else?

_____

_____

_____

_____

_____

• What survival patterns no longer serve me?

_____

_____

_____

_____

_____

- What do I want to carry forward, and what am I ready to release?

_____

_____

_____

_____

_____

Self-Compassion Challenge

Write a letter to the old version of you.

> ➤ Thank her. Mourn her. Bless her.
> ➤ Burn it (safely) or bury it under a flower.
> ➤ As you do, say: "Even when I was unraveling, I was still sacred. I wasn't broken, I was evolving."

CHAPTER
06

The Glow-Up Isn't
Always Glamorous

Croix & Solana

The Chrysalis Chronicles Continue
Glow-Up Games & Glitter Lies

A soul-fable featuring truths we pretend not to tell

Setting: Where healing is less sparkle and selfies, and more sweat, solitude, and sacred mess.

*I*t was "Glow-Up Night" at the Gathering of Great Thinkers, and the forest was LIT. Literally. Bioluminescent vines wrapped every tree like runway lights, and the vibe was somewhere between a vision board party and a TED Talk hosted by Beyoncé.

Croix the Chameleon showed up in gold lamé pants and a crown made of recycled compliments.

"I'm in my elevation era," he declared. "Healed, hydrated, and high-vibrational."

Solana side-eyed him from across the clearing, wearing no makeup, a robe, and clarity. "You moisturized, not transformed," she muttered.

Zephyr Blaze descended on a confetti wind. "Baby, if your glow-up don't involve therapy, shadow work, and crying on the kitchen floor, is it even real?"

Bella Boom tossed her wig labeled "Progress" onto a log. "Let's talk about the glow-down that had to happen before the glow-up even began."

Sir Katticus Flame added, "A true glow-up isn't the glitter. It's the guts. It's choosing alignment over applause."

And Nixie Starfire, blazing in bare feet and wisdom, said, "The most sacred glow comes in the dark, when no one's watching and you still choose yourself."

Croix blinked. "So... no celebratory selfie?"

Solana smirked, stepped into the moonlight, and said, "This glow? It cost me peace, pride, and people. And I paid in full."

Moral

The glow-up isn't always visible. Sometimes it's just choosing not to answer the phone when chaos calls, and peace is already in the room. Sometimes your glow-up is just hitting 'Do Not Disturb' on anything that dimmed your light.

Q&A for the Soul

- Have you ever felt pressure to "look healed" before you actually were?

_____

_____

_____

_____

_____

- What did your most transformative moments really look like?

_____

_____

_____

_____

_____

- What are you releasing that others still praise you for keeping?

_____

_____

_____

_____

_____

Ugly Cry in a Cute Era

I thought healing would look like a photoshoot.

Journaling and warm chai tea in a linen robe.

But my glow-up began in the dark.

Hair matted.

Eyes swollen.

My phone filled with unsent messages and breakup drafts I never delivered.

People kept saying, "You look great!"

But inside?

I was grieving 15 versions of myself at once.

I threw out my "cool girl" persona.

Buried my people-pleasing tendencies in the backyard.

Unfollowed an ex while crying and playing India.Arie on loop.

It wasn't cute.

It was holy.

No one posted about that part.

But that's where the magic happened.

Healing didn't feel like light.

It felt like falling apart on purpose.

There were nights I cried so hard I forgot what my voice sounded like when it wasn't trembling.

There were mornings I pulled joy over my shoulders like a coat two sizes too big.

I wasn't glowing.

I was grieving.

The version of me that smiled to survive was dying, and that death was loud.

No one tells you that the glow-up comes with funerals.

You bury friendships that no longer feed you.

You cremate coping mechanisms that once kept you warm.

You rise, but not without aching.

You shine, but not without scars.

And still... it's worth it.

Because one day you look in the mirror

and finally see yourself,

not the edited version, not the performance,

but you.

And you smile.

Because whew... she's a masterpiece.

The Glow-Up Ain't Glamorous

It wasn't the selfies
or the sun kissed reels,
It was sobbing at 3 AM
and still showing up to heal.
It was blocking the number
you still wanted to call.
It was standing in the mirror,
holding yourself like a black porcelain doll.

It was writing your worth
While your voice lost its girth
It was lighting candles
not for vibes, but survival.
It was losing people
but gaining revival.
The glow was never the glam.
It was the grit.
The grace.
The grit again.
They told me to bloom.
So, I did.
But they forgot to mention
I changed my tone, adjusted my volume, smiled through the ache.

I used to beg for crumbs.

I used to believe my worth depended on how much I could carry without complaint.

I gave.

My time. My energy. My softness. My second chances.

I gave laughter on days I had none left.

I gave silence when I should've screamed.

I gave explanations for wounds I didn't cause.

I shrank my voice so yours could echo louder.

I dimmed my light so you wouldn't feel small.

I gave grace while you gave conditions.

I gave apologies for bleeding from the cuts you swore didn't exist.

And still, you said it wasn't enough.

You called me too much and not enough in the same breath.

Needed me strong but punished me for my softness.

Wanted me quiet but craved my validation.

You clapped when I performed and vanished when I crumbled.

And I stayed.

Not because I didn't know how to leave,

But because I kept believing that if I just gave a little more

you would finally see me.

But you never did.

Because people who only love what you do for them

never learn how to love who you are.

So, I gathered the pieces I gave away.

And I stitched myself back together with truth,

with tenderness,

with the final thread of realization:

I gave, I gave, and I gave...

and that still was not enough for you.

But today

That is no longer my reflection to fix.

It is yours to face.

And I'm finally walking away

Not because I stopped loving you

But because I started loving me.

I gave. I gave. I gave.

And that still wasn't enough for you.

I gave until I was empty.

And you called it love.

The soil was heartbreak,

The rain was grief,

And the sun?

Came only after I stopped chasing shade.

But now? I give to myself first.

They told me I looked "better."

But what I really was...

Was free.

Truth Nugget

> *"This glow? It cost me peace, pride, and people. And I paid in full."*
> *– Solana*

Here's What It Means:

True transformation isn't free. You don't just wake up radiant, there's a cost: letting go of what you thought was love, what you thought was you, what you thought you needed to survive. The glow you see? It's not an accident. It's a receipt.

Why Solana Says It:

Because people love your light but don't always ask about your darkness. She's reminding herself, and others, that she earned every watt of that shine. She's not performing anymore; she's testifying.

Translation for Life

When you start to heal, it will cost you the familiar. But what you gain, peace, purpose, presence, is priceless. Don't let anyone discount your glow. They weren't there when it was dark.

Did You Know?

Butterflies emerge from their chrysalis wet, weak, and nearly blind.

They spend hours drying their wings, vulnerable and still.

No one claps.

No one posts it.

But that moment is everything.

Real glow-ups happen in the silence.

In the quiet, brave decision to keep becoming; without the applause.

You, beloved, are glowing even when it doesn't shine on camera.

The glow-up?

It's choosing yourself, even when it's messy.

Healing Reflection

Ask yourself:

> ➤ Have I been praised for my strength when I was actually suffering in silence?
> ➤ What parts of me did I bury just to be palatable?
> ➤ Do I celebrate the messy middle, or only the polished version of my progress?

Healing Whispers:

Real glow-ups don't happen under ring lights!!!
They happen in the quiet collapse, when you let go of people who loved your mask but couldn't hold your truth.
They happen when you cry so hard you forget what your own joy sounds like and still choose to believe in your resurrection.

This chapter is your permission slip to stop pretending your healing has to be pretty.
It's okay if your transformation looked like breaking before it looked like beauty.
You weren't falling apart, you were finally coming home.

Let this be your reminder:
You don't owe anyone a photo-ready version of your becoming.
Your glow is sacred, not staged.

And the most beautiful thing about you?

You kept going anyway.

This chapter also reminds us that the caterpillar dissolves before it flies. Let's tell the truth about transformation, without the Instagram filter.

Empowerment & Self-Compassion Challenge

Truth Over Trend

Affirmations

> ➤ My growth doesn't need to be pretty to be powerful.
>
> ➤ I choose substance over performance.
>
> ➤ My peace is more important than being praised.

Journaling Prompts

- What part of your healing journey didn't look "glamorous", but changed you anyway?

_____

_____

_____

_____

_____

- Where have you been pretending to glow when you're actually grieving?

_____

_____

_____

_____

_____

- What are you ready to shed, even if others still celebrate it?

_____

_____

_____

_____

_____

Self-Compassion Challenge

Take a photo of yourself with no filters, no edits.

Write a love letter to that version.

Title it: "This is What Becoming Looks Like."

CHAPTER

07

The Glow-Up Gospel

Croix & Solana

The Light Switch Lies

A Fable with Sparkle, Sass & Soul

This is where we peel back another layer of transformation and truth. Solana is glowing now, but that glow came at a cost. And guess who's back to stir things up? Our entire cast of cosmic comedic truth-slingers.

In the Midnight Garden, where luminous fireflies float like spotlights and truth clings to the vines, and healing speaks louder than apologies. Solana stood center stage under a silver-dipped moon, radiant from root to wing. Her glow wasn't just seen, it was felt. Solana stood still. Her wings, dipped in gold and resilience, glowed from a joy no man had given her, and none could dim. She didn't just arrive; she radiated.

She had the kind of glow that doesn't ask for permission. The kind you earn after surviving the dark and daring to laugh anyway. The tips of her wings shimmered with gold dust and self-respect. She wore peace like perfume, and freedom like a tailored suit.

Then came that sound, the rustle of a snake in sequins.

Croix the Chameleon slinked out from behind a moon-kissed willow, holding a bouquet of borrowed lines and recycled charm. His colors flickered nervously between nostalgia and regret.

Wearing a grin, his eyes widened as they caught the shimmer of her presence.
"Look at you, Solana… you're luminous," he murmured, that old tone laced with awe and a touch of regret. "You're out here radiating like a whole solar flare," he said, blinking like her glow came with a sunburn warning. "You're really glowing now," he whispered, in a low and familiar voice, like a memory dressed in yesterday's cologne.

Solana turned, her face calm and knowing. "I've been shining," she replied coolly. "You just had your sunglasses on."
Just then, Zephyr Blaze descended in a cloud of bubblegum-scented smoke and holographic feathers, his glitter heels clicking like exclamation points. He gave Solana a wink before turning his gaze to Croix. "Isn't it wild," he said with a twirl, "how folks find your number the second you delete theirs?"

Laughter floated in on the breeze as Bella Boom made her entrance, hips swaying like the truth. She carried a martini glass filled with herbal tea, lashes long enough to brush off bad energy. "Let me guess," she said, taking a sip.

"He misses her 'energy' now that she glowed up?"

A velvet chaise lounge scraped gently along the moss as Sir Katticus Flame appeared, cosmic cocoa in hand, his eyes glimmering with wit. "Every time a butterfly glows," he said, settling in with a sigh, "a chameleon gets insecure. It's science."

From the treetops, a cascade of glitter signaled the arrival of Nixie Starfire. With stardust in her hair and side-eye sharper than a sword, she floated down and whispered, "If he wanted to be part of your healing, baby... he wouldn't have been the wound."

Solana didn't flinch. She didn't recoil or question. She smiled, not the polite, practiced one she used to give out freely, but a soft, sacred one that bloomed from within.

Croix took a step forward, reaching out, as if her light somehow gave him permission to return.

But Solana lifted her hand gently, like a traffic cop in Chanel, and stopped him mid-sentence.

"This light," she said, voice like silk with steel underneath, "is mine. Not a porchlight. Not a trap. Not a test. Just... me."

Croix blinked. There was silence. Croix blinked again.

The garden fell into a hush, the kind of silence that doesn't ask for answers. Solana turned and walked toward the starlit archway ahead, her glow trailing behind like a blessing she gave to herself. And the others? They didn't follow. They simply cheered.

> ## Moral
>
> A glow-up is not a green light for ghosts. Just because someone sees your worth now doesn't mean they're worthy of it.
> Protect your peace.
> It's not petty; it's called keeping your space holy.
> Not everyone clapping for your glow-up wants to see you shine.
> But baby, glow anyway.

Q&A for the Soul

- Who tries to re-enter your life now that you're glowing?

_____

_____

_____

_____

- What part of you used to dim so others could stay comfortable?

_____

_____

_____

_____

- How do you protect your light without apologizing for it?

_____

_____

_____

_____

When I Got My Glow Back

I used to think peace was a place I had to earn.

That joy came only after pain, and confidence only came with someone else's approval.

But peace isn't a destination.

It's a decision.

There was a time I would've answered the phone for anyone who hurt me, if they called with a sad enough voice.

But now?

I let it ring.

Because peace doesn't need closure. It needs boundaries.

I got my glow back, not from revenge, not from validation, but from coming home to myself.

And once you glow from the inside out?

Baby, there isn't a chameleon alive who can dim you.

She Glowed Anyway

They told her she was "too much."

So, she became more.

They said,

"Tone it down."

She turned it up.

Softer didn't save her.

Quieter didn't shield her.

Smaller didn't love her.

So, she stopped shrinking.

Started glowing.

Even in the dark.

Especially in the dark.

Truth Nugget

> *"This light is mine. Not a porchlight. Not a trap. Not a test. Just... me."*
> **– Solana**

Here's What It Means:

This declaration isn't just poetic, it's revolutionary.

So often, women are taught to shrink their shine or to make it useful for others:

To attract,

To rescue,

To prove they're "worthy" of love.

But Solana's words reclaim radiance as sovereignty, not strategy.

She is not glowing to invite him back.

She is glowing because she finally stopped dimming.

Why the Character Says It:

In this moment, Solana has fully stepped into her healing.

Croix, like many- shapeshifters before him, appears right when she's rising, suddenly remembering her number once she's deleted his.

He thinks her glow is a signal, a flicker of invitation.

But Solana draws the line. With grace. With steel.

She doesn't shout. She doesn't need to.

This isn't revenge. It's a boundary wrapped in brilliance.

Did You Know?

Butterflies don't return to the cocoon.

They don't ask permission to evolve.

And they don't dim their wings to comfort caterpillars.

Your glow-up isn't arrogance.

It's arrival.

Translation for Life:

Too often, our radiance becomes performative, we shine so they'll stay.

This truth nugget reminds us:

You're allowed to evolve without explaining it to those who misused the older version of you.

Your growth isn't bait.

Your joy isn't an apology.

Your healing isn't an open door for those who hurt you.

Solana's light is not a lighthouse for lost causes.

It is the natural glow of someone who survived herself.

Healing Reflection

Ask yourself:

> ➢ Who tries to interpret your healing as an invitation?
> ➢ What parts of your glow do you still feel guilty about?
> ➢ Can you let your light be just yours, no performance, no pressure?

Let Solana's words echo in your spirit:

"This light is mine."

Not a porchlight waiting for anyone to come home.

Not a trap to teach anyone a lesson.

Not a test to see if they've changed.

Just… a glow reborn, healing, and choosing herself again and again.

Empowerment & Self-Compassion Challenge The Glow-Up Protocol

Affirmations

> ➤ I don't owe anyone access to me.
> ➤ My glow is not a group project.
> ➤ My glow is a divine design.
> ➤ I do not fear being too much.
> ➤ I do not fear having an overflow.
> ➤ I am flowing into the divine design of me.
> ➤ I am who I was born to be.

Journaling Prompts

• Who do you still dim your light around, and why?

_____

_____

_____

_____

_____

- What's one part of yourself you reclaimed after leaving someone who didn't deserve you?

_____

_____

_____

_____

_____

- What does your glow-up look like emotionally, spiritually, physically?

_____

_____

_____

_____

_____

Self-Compassion Challenge

Stand in front of a mirror tonight and look yourself in the eyes and say:

"This is who I've become, and I am beautiful, brilliant, and worthy of every single blessing on the way."

CHAPTER
08

Wings Made of Wisdom

Croix & Solana

The Parables Continue
"Wings Made of Wisdom"

A Fable of Sacred Growth, Confetti Healing & Unapologetic Joy

he Gathering had ended. The vines were quiet. The truth-flowers had folded for the night. And Solana? She wasn't at any moonlit soiree or healing circle. She was home.

Her own sacred space.

Incense burning. Jazz low. Edges laid.

This was the part they don't show, the joy after the crying, the silly dance break after the breakthrough, the soul giggles that sneak in when you realize:

You survived. And not only that, you're shining again.

Suddenly, a knock.

Croix stood on the porch with his "Reformed Man Starter Pack", therapy buzzwords and a reusable tote of regrets.

"You look... different," he said.

"Peaceful. Like you finally healed."

"You're glowing now.

I mean, really glowing.

Like... I don't even know how to explain it."

He chuckled, soft and stunned.

"It's like you bottled up every sunrise you ever cried through and made it shine back."

He blinked again, slower this time.

"I did," Solana replied, sipping tea. "But you didn't think healing meant I'd want you back, did you?"

Zephyr Blaze floated in through the window like incense smoke with sparkles.

"Baby, there's nothin' more beautiful than a woman who glows for herself. You better sip that tea and let that man simmer in his almost!"

Bella Boom burst through the back door with a charcuterie board of affirmations.

"Let's toast to this glow," she said, "because honey, joy looks good on you."

Sir Katticus reclined across the couch like a velvet sermon.

"True confidence is quiet," he meowed.
"But it will still clear a room of people who prefer your broken pieces."

And from the bookshelf came a burst of stardust, Nixie Starfire, twirling midair, whispering:
"You stopped trying to be understood and started being at peace. That's not ego. That's evolution."

Solana smiled.
Not because she needed validation,
But because she no longer craved permission.
Her wings didn't flap for applause.
They fluttered for freedom.

Moral
When healing becomes your home, not a performance, you stop flying for validation and start soaring for joy. True growth isn't loud, it glows. And joy? It doesn't need a witness to be real.

Q&A for the Soul

- When was the last time you felt joy without guilt?

_____

_____

_____

_____

_____

- What does embodied confidence feel like to you, physically, spiritually, emotionally?

_____

_____

_____

_____

_____

- What would it look like to define "healing" in your own words, not theirs?

_____

_____

_____

_____

_____

Joy Came Back Softly

There was no trumpet.

No big moment.

Just a small shift.

A Saturday morning, unbothered.

A belly laugh at a silly meme.

A slow sip of tea with no sense of urgency.

I realized one day that joy had returned, not as a celebration, but as a roommate.

No longer something I had to chase, but something I remembered how to welcome.

Healing didn't shout. It whispered.

"You're safe now."

The Soft Return

She didn't come back loud,
She came back soft.
In the hush between to-do lists,
In the sigh after a long bath.
She returned in the taste of a ripe peach,
The way morning sunlight wrapped her shoulders.
Joy didn't knock.
She let herself in.

Truth Nugget

"You stopped trying to be understood and started being at peace."
– Nixie Starfire

Here's What It Means:

Letting go of the need for approval isn't apathy, it's evolution.
It means you've moved from seeking validation to honoring your truth. Peace no longer depends on anyone else's comprehension.

Did You Know?

Butterfly Brains

Butterflies don't forget; especially Monarchs. They retain memory from their caterpillar days.

Some species of butterflies form lifelong mating pairs based on trust signals, chemical and behavioral. Scientists have observed that butterflies remember pain, avoid toxic patterns, and adapt their behavior after trauma.

Why the Character Says It:

Nixie Starfire, half-stardust and all wisdom, recognizes when Solana crosses the threshold into wholeness. She celebrates not just survival, but the embodiment of growth, the part where you don't have to explain your wings to anyone.

Translation for Life

Butterflies can remember who hurt them. Monarchs can recall the scent of danger from when they were caterpillars. Butterflies don't return to what once harmed them. Neither should we. That means they can remember trauma and still fly.

So can you!

Let this remind you: Healing isn't erasure. It's integration. And joy isn't forgetting, it's in spite of.

Stop begging people to understand your healing, your decisions, your joy.

Not everyone gets a front-row seat to your resurrection.

Live anyway.

Glow anyway.

Healing Reflection

Ask yourself:

> ➤ Am I glowing for myself or still performing for applause?
> ➤ What does peace actually feel like in my body, not just in theory, but in practice?
> ➤ What parts of me are finally safe to take up space again?

Healing Whispers

Healing doesn't always arrive in big, cinematic moments.

Sometimes, it slips in like sunlight on clean sheets.

Sometimes, it hums in your laughter, bubbles in your tea, dances in the ordinary.

This chapter is your reminder that joy is not a reward for suffering.

It is your birthright.

You don't owe anyone an explanation for your glow, especially not the ones who only cheered when you were dim.

You've reclaimed your wings.

And these wings?

They don't flutter for attention.

They fly for freedom.

They carry you to soft mornings, sacred boundaries, and the kind of peace that doesn't need permission.

Let this be your sacred yes:

You are no longer surviving, you're soaring.

Empowerment & Self-Compassion Challenge

Affirmations

- ➤ My joy is sacred and doesn't need an audience.
- ➤ I choose peace over performance.
- ➤ I am not here to be understood, I am here to be whole.
- ➤ I radiate love without losing myself.

Journaling Prompts

- Describe a moment when you felt joy just for yourself.

_____

_____

_____

_____

_____

- Whose misunderstanding have you carried for too long?

_____

_____

_____

_____

_____

- Write a love letter to your healed self. Include the mundane magic she deserves.

_____

_____

_____

_____

_____

Self-Compassion Challenge

Put on your favorite feel-good playlist.

Dance like nobody's disappointed.

Move like someone who knows their joy is holy.

CHAPTER
09

The Garden Within

Croix & Solana

The Chrysalis Chronicles Continue
"The Garden Within"

A sacred fable rooted in rest, reverence, and the art of not answering old doors

*I*n a hidden clearing surrounded by whispering willows and moon-bathed marigolds, Solana was found tending to something quiet, her peace. No spotlights. No stage. Just stillness.

She had built a garden no one could enter without her invitation. The soil was soft with self-compassion, and the fence was made of boundaries no longer barbed with guilt.

Croix, now draped in faux humility and carrying a bouquet of half-apologies, stood just beyond the archway.

"Solana," he said, his voice laced with old rhythms. "You always kept a good heart."

She didn't turn. She was pruning silence. Cultivating ease.
"You always knew how to make things beautiful," he added.

Solana finally looked up, her eyes a mirror of the moon. "Yes," she replied gently. "And now, I know how to keep them safe."

From behind a magnolia tree, Zephyr Blaze peeked out and gasped theatrically. "Oooh, she locked the gate and kept the key! Look at her, blooming and boundary-bound!"
Bella Boom, lounging in a hammock of rose petals, sipped jasmine tea and declared, "That's not just healing, baby. That's interior design for the soul."

Sir Katticus, sharpening his claws on a bamboo scroll, chimed in. "Let the record reflect, there's nothing stronger than a woman who can choose peace over performance."

And Nixie Starfire, twirling slowly in a spiral of sage and sound bowls, whispered, "The world will keep knocking. But now... she answers only to herself."

Croix blinked. The wind did not respond. Solana returned to her garden, unfazed.

Moral

When you build peace within, even the noisiest pasts lose their power. Not everything that calls you deserves an answer.

Q&A for the Soul

- What does "the garden within" mean to you? Is it a physical place, a state of mind, or a boundary you've built? Describe what your inner garden looks like, and who or what is no longer allowed inside.

_____

_____

_____

_____

_____

- Have you ever answered a 'door' that should've stayed closed? What old rhythms still try to knock, and how can you practice saying no without guilt?

_____

_____

_____

_____

_____

- What does peace actually feel like in your body? Is it silence? Softness? Strength? How can you start choosing it more often, even in small ways?

  _____

  _____

  _____

  _____

  _____

- What boundaries do you need to protect your peace, emotionally, digitally, or energetically? Who drains your soil? What replenishes it?

  _____

  _____

  _____

  _____

  _____

- Solana didn't explain. She didn't defend. She just returned to tending her peace. What would it look like for you to stop over-explaining and start simply being?

  _____

  _____

  _____

"Sanctuary"

There was a time I mistook busyness for purpose.

I filled my life with people, projects, and noise,

Not realizing I was running from the quiet that held my healing.

I let too many voices in.

Too many opinions rearranged my insides.

I forgot what my own peace sounded like.

But there came a season when I craved stillness more than validation.

I stopped explaining myself.

I stopped opening the door for chaos dressed in nostalgia.

And I started tending to the space within me that felt like home.

Now?

I bloom where I am rooted.

And not everyone gets a tour.

"No Entry Without Invitation"

I planted peace like wildflowers,
in places once scorched by betrayal.
I guarded my time
like sacred soil,
my joy like ripe fruit not for plucking.
There was no neon sign.
No buzzer.
No welcome mat.
Just soft light,
a locked gate,
and a sign that read:
"If you come with chaos, don't."

Truth Nugget

"The world will keep knocking. But now... she answers only to herself."
– *Nixie Starfire*

Here's What It Means:

This is about reclaiming your agency. When you've done the work to heal, you no longer owe your attention, affection, or access to everyone who wants it.

Did You Know?

Butterflies are drawn to calm, sunny gardens, especially those rich in nectar and free of toxins.
Just like humans, they thrive best in places that nourish, not drain them.

Let that remind you:
You don't owe access to anyone who poisons your peace.

Why the Character Says It:

Nixie is the guardian of radiance and intuition. She sees how many people confuse compassion with compliance. Her line is a celebration of self-honoring choices.

Translation for Life:

Boundaries aren't walls.

They're sacred invitations. And not everyone qualifies for an entry; especially those who once trampled your garden.

Healing Reflection

Ask yourself:

- ➢ Who do I still feel obligated to let in, even when my spirit says no?
- ➢ What parts of my peace feel most vulnerable when the past knocks?
- ➢ Where in my life am I being called to prune, not perform?

Healing Whispers:

Peace is not passive.

It is not accidental.

It is cultivated, shovelful by shovelful, breath by breath.

Healing is not just about what you release, but who you protect it from afterward.

Boundaries aren't punishments.

They're preservation.

They're the invisible fences that say:

"I am no longer available for anything that makes me forget my worth."

Your inner garden is holy ground.

And just because someone once walked through it… doesn't mean they still deserve a key.

Remember, you do not have to explain your gate, your growth, or your glow.

You've earned your sanctuary.
Now protect it like your joy depends on it, because it does.

Empowerment & Self-Compassion Challenge

Affirmations

> ➤ I do not open my gate for ghosts.
> ➤ I protect my peace with softness and strength.
> ➤ I am not cold, I am clear.
> ➤ My presence is a privilege, not a default.

Journaling Prompts

- Where do I need to reclaim silence in my life?

_____

_____

_____

_____

_____

- What old door am I tempted to open again, and why?

_____

_____

_____

_____

_____

- Describe your "inner garden." What does it need to thrive?

_____

_____

_____

_____

_____

Self-Compassion Challenge

Build a "peace list": light a candle, sit in silence, and breathe into your body. Write a list of people or habits who no longer belong in your garden. Burn the list. Let it become compost for your future joy.

CHAPTER
10

The Chameleon Returns

Croix & Solana

The Last Mask Falls

A Fable of Full Circle, Boundaries, and the Butterfly's Crown

The garden was different now.

It no longer whispered warnings, it sang.

Truth grew like wildflowers. Self-worth floated like pollen in the breeze.

And Solana?

She didn't just fly.

She soared like she had ancestors tucked under her wings.

That's when Croix returned.

Soft-shoed and smooth-talking, as if regret were perfume.

"Whoa… Solana," he breathed, his eyes tracking the light that danced along her shoulders. "You look… luminous. And I don't even think it's the light. I think it's you."

"I came to make it right," he said, holding out the same hands that once dimmed her light.

Solana turned slowly. Not startled. Not shaken.

She was sunrise in slow motion. All brilliance and no apology.

"You came to make peace with your guilt," she said.

"But I already made peace with myself."

Zephyr Blaze somersaulted out of a tree, landing in a cloud of biodegradable glitter.

"Baby, she doesn't wear the same soul size anymore! You're have to go shop in the clearance section of your own healing!"

Bella Boom sashayed past, sunglasses shaped like no's.

"If he missed your magic, tell him to book a ticket to used to be. This woman? She's walkin' in 'won't ever again.'"

Sir Katticus Flame meowed from a perch above.

"The final test is never the villain. It's your reaction. And she just passed with honors."

Then Nixie Starfire fluttered down, glowing like truth wrapped in tenderness.

"You're not being tested to go back. You're being shown how far you've come."

Solana smiled, not because she needed to prove anything,

but because she had nothing left to hide.

She didn't owe Croix closure.

She didn't owe anyone access.

Solana tilted her head slightly, the corner of her mouth lifting, not in flirtation, but in clarity. In peace.

"This glow?" she said, her voice soft but unmistakable. "It came from the ashes. Not applause."

She didn't step closer. She didn't shrink or sway. She just stood there, whole.

"You're seeing me now," she continued, "but I've been becoming her this whole time."

Around them, the Midnight Garden pulsed. Not louder, but deeper. Like the earth itself was exhaling with her.

Zephyr Blaze, watching from the archway of moon-blooms, whispered to Bella Boom,

"Oop. Somebody better call NASA 'because she just eclipsed his whole illusion."

Bella nodded, adjusting her crown made of past red flags.

"And she didn't even raise her voice. That's a grown woman glow."

With a wink and a halo full of stardust, Nixie cackled,

"Somebody call tech support, his ego just crashed into her boundaries."

Sir Katticus stirred his cosmic cocoa and sighed,

"That wasn't a walk away. That was a cosmic unfollow. She upgraded from 'us' to 'universe'.

There's no magic like rising magic.

Especially when she no longer needs the audience."

And Solana?

She looked out over the garden.

Then she turned her gaze toward the stars, not the shadow behind her.

With a voice woven from closure and clarity, she whispered, not to him, but to her healing:

"Let this be the last time I ever shrink to fit someone else's blindness."

"I'm not who you remember," she said gently.

"I'm who I fought to become."

Croix blinked. And blinked again.

The final blink.

And this time?

She didn't just fly away.

She rose.

Crowned.

Laughing.

Glowing.

Her joy didn't just glow, it echoed.

When the familiar comes knocking in a new disguise,

you don't shrink, shapeshift, or silence your light.

You don't explain the glow you earned in the dark.

You've become the someone who doesn't flinch, doesn't fold, and

doesn't audition for love you already carry within.

This time, you don't just rise.

You soar, wings unapologetic, joy undeniable, peace untouchable.

Moral

The final test isn't their return, it's your remembrance because real love won't make your glow a problem or your peace a negotiation. Anything less? Return to sender.

Q&A for the Soul

- When did you last realize you'd outgrown your old wounds?

_____

_____

_____

_____

_____

- Who still expects the version of you that no longer exists?

_____

_____

_____

_____

- What does it feel like to be free?

_____

_____

_____

_____

Memoir: "When Joy Became My Glow"

There was a version of me who answered late-night texts.

Who said yes when she meant maybe.

Who apologized for her glow.

But that version wept so I could rise.

And now, when peace calls, I answer on the first ring.

Joy didn't arrive like a parade.

It arrived like a quiet morning,

No makeup. No filter. Just me.

Still here. Still soft. Still sacred.

But now?

Unshakable.

"I Don't Blend Anymore"

She used to blend,
Like storm light in still water.
Like lullabies in rooms with closed
doors. But now?
She walks in as gospel.
She exits like thunder.
She laughs full-bodied,
And writes her name in fireflies.
She left the garden
But took the seeds.
She doesn't blend in anymore,
She blooms.

Truth Nugget

"You're not being tested to go back. You're being shown how far you've come."
– Nixie Starfire

Here's What It Means:

Growth isn't about resisting old temptation.

It's about recognizing that it no longer fits.

The test isn't about them. It's about you.

Did You Know?

Butterflies see ultraviolet colors.

Their world is brighter than ours.

They literally live in light we can't see.

And once they fly,

they never return to the cocoon.

Because the cocoon was just the waiting room for more greatness.

Why the Character Says It:

Nixie Starfire has always been Solana's inner compass. She appears when Solana's heart needs clarity. This time, she arrives not to warn, but to witness. Because Solana's already passed. The glow-up is complete.

Translation for Life:

When the old version of you gets tested, remember:
You are not in the same chapter.
You are the author now.
Turn the page.

Healing Reflection

Ask yourself:

> ➢ Who still calls out to the version of me I buried with grace?
>
> ➢ Do I trust myself enough to not open the door, even when the knock is familiar?
>
> ➢ How does it feel to wear peace like perfume, instead of proving it with words?

Healing Whispers:

You don't owe anyone the parts of you that had to die so you could live whole.

You've already done the work, the crying, the craving, the climbing.

And now? You don't shrink when they show up.

You remember. You rise.

Let this reflection remind you:

You are not a test to be passed.

You are the result.

The revelation.

The rebirth.

No more rehearsing worthiness for those who missed the masterpiece.

Your glow is not on trial.

It is the truth.

And this time, beloved, you don't blend in.

You bless the ground you walk on.

Joy Glow

The Anthem.
The Arrival.
The After.
Joy Glow is the fire that clawed its way
through rain and rubble.
The ember that outlived the storm.
The laugh that broke through tears you thought
would never end.
The mirror that finally shows a face you recognize,
not broken, but blazing.

It is the red lipstick you put on for your own reflection.
The song that thunders in your ribs when the room goes quiet.
The quiet dance in your kitchen that feels like a coronation.

Joy Glow is healing that still carries a scar.
It is scars that sing instead of shame.
It is boundaries that glitter like jeweled armor.
It is smiling while saying no, and never flinching.
It is whispering "I deserve this"
and hearing your soul answer back, "Exactly."

It is peace that drowns out the crowd.
It is reclaiming your story from the Chameleon's venom,

not to spit it back,
but to rise above it.
Because this is not revenge.
This is resurrection.

Joy Glow is her.
The woman they tried to shrink.
The one they told, "Stay small."
But she spread.
She rose.
She stretched wide.
She unfolded.
She found her wings.

Joy Glow is you.
Not broken.
Not surviving.
Arrived.
Home.
Crowned in courage.
Draped in grace.
Anointed in fire.

You did not just come back.
You came back as the sunrise no storm could kill.
Battle-tested.

Heart-protected.
Soul-resurrected.

And now?
You are the storm.
You are the sunrise.
You are the prayer and the proof.
The encore and the standing ovation.

And the world?
They do not just watch.
They rise when you enter.

Joy Glow is you.
Unapologetic.
Unshaken.
Undeniable.
Not just home.
But the whole horizon.

And baby,
you do not just light it up.
You set the sky on fire.

Empowerment & Self-Compassion Challenge

Affirmations

> ➤ I am the closure I once craved.
> ➤ My joy is not dependent on return texts or old apologies.
> ➤ I don't blend in. I radiate.
> ➤ I celebrate myself Loudly, Beautifully, Endlessly.

Journaling Prompts

- What does "Joy Glow" mean to you today?

_____

_____

_____

_____

_____

- What chapter of your life are you ready to end with a celebration?

_____

_____

_____

_____

_____

- Write the first sentence of your next season.

_____

_____

_____

_____

_____

Self-Compassion Challenge

Create a "Glow-Up Legacy List":

- ➢ 10 things you've let go of
- ➢ 10 things you've reclaimed
- ➢ 10 things you're creating next

Then?

Dance.

Laugh.

Share this book with someone who's ready to rise.

"Wings After the War"

Her wings were not the same,
they were brighter.
Not because they were untouched,
but because they had been broken,
burned by betrayal,
and still found their way to beauty.
Each tear stitched with truth.
Each crack painted in perseverance.
They glowed not in spite of the damage,
but because of it.
Once pastel, now powerful,
saturated with sacredness.
You see, healing doesn't return you to who you were.
It transforms you into who you were always meant to be.
And her wings?
They didn't just flutter.
They roared.

Why Solana's Wings Shine Brighter Now

Scientifically speaking, butterfly wings are made of tiny overlapping scales that refract and reflect light. After damage, some butterflies develop bolder colorations as a defense mechanism, or due to environmental triggers that shift pigmentation or light diffusion.

Symbolically, Solana's post-healing wings are a metaphor for post-traumatic growth: the psychological phenomenon where individuals become more resilient, empathetic, and purpose-driven after adversity.

So yes, her wings are more radiant now.
Because they've weathered storms, survived molting seasons, and appeared with wisdom woven into every thread.

CHAPTER
11

The Company You Keep

Croix & Solana

The Cast That Stayed
"The Garden Table"

A Soul-Tale of Seats, Seasons, and the Friends That Feed You

In the heart of the Midnight Garden, Solana set a table, not a throne. No velvet ropes. No hierarchy. Just cushions of truth and laughter under moonlight.

Zephyr Blaze popped a squat on a cushion shaped like a shooting star.

"Look at this setup! No drama, no auditions, just vibes and vegan cheese."

Bella Boom strutted in late, but radiant.

"Honey, she's not building walls.

She's planting rose bushes with guest lists."

Sir Katticus Flame adjusted his monocle fashioned out of a teacup handle.

"Let the record show, a wise woman curates her company like she curates her peace."

Nixie Starfire floated down with a tray of soul snacks. "Your healing?"

"It needs witnesses."

"And some of 'em better come with glitter and grit."

Solana looked around the table. No one here asked her to dim. No one here flinched at her shadow or feared her shine. These weren't just friends. These were anchors in the storm and amplifiers in the light.

Just then, a knock echoed from the garden gate. A familiar rhythm. Croix. Again.

Zephyr peeked through the vines.

"It's giving... recycled plot twist."

Bella Boom sipped her tea with a side-eye.

"If he didn't bring soul food for the table, baby, we're not making room."

Sir Katticus sharpened his wit.

"We don't entertain ghosts at dinner. Only guests."

And Nixie? She lit a candle and whispered,

"When your circle reflects your worth, you stop arguing with the echoes of who you used to be."

Solana didn't get up.

She didn't even look.

She just passed the joy bowl to Zephyr and laughed from a place that echoed.

Not everyone deserves a seat.

And that's not bitterness.

That's blooming with boundaries.

Moral

True friendship is a feast of soul food.

Not every knock

Deserves an open door.

Peace is the password and not everyone earns the feast of your light.

So, share your bread only with those who water your roots.

Q&A for the Soul

- Who at your table pours back into you?

_____

_____

_____

_____

- Are you surrounded by people who clap when you grow, or just when you stay the same?

_____

_____

_____

_____

- What boundaries need to be planted around your joy?

_____

_____

_____

_____

Memoir Moment: "Those Who Clapped in the Dark"

There was a time I mistook presence for support.

If someone stayed, I assumed they cared.

But some just lingered to study your softness... or steal your spotlight.

The ones who mattered didn't just show up at the book launch,

They were the ones reading rough drafts when I wanted to give up.

The ones holding mirrors when I forgot my glow.

Now?

I choose the ones who feed my soul, not my fear.

I don't audition for love.

And I don't confuse history with harmony.

"Seats at the Soul Table"

Some came hungry,
but left crumbs.
Some came loud,
but never listened.
And then…
Some showed up soft,
with full hearts and empty hands,
ready to pour, ready to witness,
ready to grow with you.
Keep those ones.
The ones who clap when you're quiet.
The ones who hold space,
not scorecards.
Your glow deserves a guest list.

Truth Nugget

"When your circle reflects your worth, you stop arguing with the echoes of who you used to be."
— Nixie Starfire

What It Means:

Healing doesn't require isolation, but it does require discernment. Your glow needs guardians, not just guests.

Did You Know?

Your nervous system can mirror the energy of your inner circle.

Studies in neuroscience show that humans possess "mirror neurons," which allow us to subconsciously mimic and absorb the emotions, behaviors, and even stress levels of those around us. This is why being in the presence of calm, supportive people can actually regulate your nervous system while being around chaotic or critical people can increase anxiety, self-doubt, and emotional dysregulation.

Why Nixie Says It:

She's the spirit of intuition and inner truth. Nixie reminds us that not everyone clapping is celebrating, and not everyone silent is against us. Real ones feel you without fanfare.

Translation for Life:

Audit your circle. Your energy is currency. Spend it where love doesn't cost your peace.

The people you surround yourself with don't just influence your mood, they help shape your healing.

Healing often begins where you are seen, celebrated, and safe to be your full self.

Every healing journey needs a crew, because wholeness is a team effort.

In storytelling and psychology, supporting characters often represent internal voices or emotional archetypes, courage, intuition, humor, wisdom. Solana's circle isn't just entertainment. It's emotional architecture.

Zephyr Blaze brings levity and truth. Bella Boom models boundaries and boldness. Sir Katticus embodies discernment and loyalty. Nixie Starfire whispers intuition and grace.

Together, they reflect the soul's support system, the cheerleaders, truth-tellers, and quiet guardians we all deserve.

Sometimes, the best version of you is revealed through the people who see you clearly, love you loudly, and remind you to keep glowing.

Did You Know?

Chosen family can rewire your sense of safety and self-worth.

Psychological studies show that a consistent, affirming support system, what many call "chosen family," can repair attachment wounds, increase resilience, and provide the emotional safety that may have been missing in early life. Unlike biological ties, chosen family is built on shared values, mutual respect, and love without conditions.

Empowerment & Self-Compassion Challenge

Affirmation

> ➤ I attract aligned souls who celebrate my shine, respect my peace, and walk with me in purpose. I release all that drains and embrace what sustains.

Journal Prompt

- Who are my soul-keepers, the ones who water my joy, reflect my truth, and make room for my evolution?

_____

_____

_____

_____

_____

The Circle That Holds You

Healing isn't always a solo act, sometimes it's a soul symphony. A soul doesn't heal in isolation. It blooms in community.

According to relational neuroscience, co-regulation is how we calm, grow, and thrive through safe connections.

When you're surrounded by people who see your light (even on your dim days), your nervous system learns safety, joy, and trust again.

Solana's crew isn't just comic relief, they represent the emotional tools every butterfly needs:

> ➢ Zephyr Blaze: Joyful honesty and hype-man energy
> ➢ Bella Boom: Boundaries with a side of beauty and sass
> ➢ Sir Katticus Flame: Loyalty, instinct, and quiet clarity
> ➢ Nixie Starfire: Inner knowing, spiritual grace, and intuition

In every season of glow-up, your circle shapes your safety. Choose the ones who water your wings.

Journal Prompt: "Who's in Your Garden?"

Take a moment to reflect on the people who nurture you, the ones who water your roots instead of stealing your sunlight. Let your answers be honest and unfiltered, this is your space.

- Who in your life brings you clarity, not confusion?

_____

_____

_____

_____

_____

- Who respects your growth and reflects your truth?

_____

_____

_____

_____

_____

- What kind of friend are you to others on their healing path?

_____

_____

_____

_____

_____

- Where do you need more Zephyr? More Bella? More Nixie?

_____

_____

_____

_____

_____

- What kind of support system are you ready to build or refine?

_____

_____

_____

_____

_____

Character Reflection

Solana's Circle of Light

Solana didn't rise because she was alone, she rose because she was held.

Every soul needs a circle that won't let them shrink. That says, "You don't have to explain your glow, we've been rooting for it." Her crew didn't rescue her; they reminded her.

And isn't that the most sacred kind of friendship?
The ones who don't flinch when you evolve.
The ones who hand you the crown you forgot you were already wearing.

The ones who say, "You don't need us to shine, but we'll be here dancing in your light anyway."

Dear Butterfly,

You made it. You turned every page, held your breath through the ache, whispered yes through the truth, and kept going; even when it stung a little too close to the bone. And now… here you are. Not the same as when you began. Softer, maybe. Stronger, definitely. Wiser in the ways that don't always show on the outside, but radiate like a quiet sunrise from the inside.

You've read the parables. Felt the ache. Reclaimed your wings. This is your permission slip to rise; even when it's messy. Especially when it's messy.

You don't owe the world perfection. You don't need anyone's permission to bloom. You are not required to shrink to be loved, or to explain your light to those who prefer the dark.

Let this be your confirmation: You have permission to evolve. You are allowed to protect your peace like a rare flower. You are allowed to be joyful, radiant, and whole, even with a past that tried to fracture you. Let this be the note you hum when you are done reading this:

- ➢ Your healing is sacred.
- ➢ Your softness is not weakness.
- ➢ Your story is not shame.
- ➢ Your voice is a miracle.

And your glow?

It's not a phase.

It's a homecoming.

You are the proof. The poetry. The power.

You are the one your younger self prayed for.

And now, the world gets to see you fly. Not because you needed to be saved, but because you finally saw your own wings.

With all the love, glitter, and grace I can hold,

V. Morgan

Your sister in flight, your sister in the chrysalis, your companion in the glow

She Doesn't Blend in Anymore

*S*he used to shrink to be safe.
Now she expands to be sacred.
She used to whisper her truth.
Now her story sings in full color.

Solana no longer asks for permission to glow.
She simply does.
She flies in full bloom, not waiting to be chosen,
but choosing herself daily.
Croix may return. Old patterns may knock.
But the woman she is now?
She opens the door, not with fear, but with discernment.
She remembers the branch that broke her.
She also remembers she doesn't need branches
anymore. She's sky bound.

Final Blessing

"*Be as a lamp unto them that walk in darkness, a joy to the sorrowful, a sea for the thirsty, a haven for the distressed, an upholder and defender of the victim of oppression.*"

– *Bahá'u'lláh*

Beloved soul, may your journey never be hidden under a bushel, but may it shine like a lamp upon the hills.

May your light reach those who walk in darkness, offering them hope. May your joy be a balm for the sorrowful, your love a sea for the thirsty, your heart a haven for the distressed, and your courage a shield for the oppressed.

And may the words of Christ echo through your days:

"*Let your light so shine before men, that they may see your good works, and glorify your Father which is in heaven.*"

– **Matthew 5:16 (KJV)**

Go forth in peace. Walk in power. Stand in love.

And may your wings, made of wisdom, forged in fire, and kissed by grace, carry you into every tomorrow with strength, beauty, and unshakable light.

Glowing Bonus Materials

Glossary of Toxic Tricks

The Language of Manipulation

These are the red flags dressed in charm, confusion, and chaos.

TERM	DEFINITION
Gaslighting	When someone makes you question your reality, your memory, or your truth. *Translation:* You're certain the sky is blue, but they'll argue it's green until you're squinting at the clouds, wondering if you've lost it. **Bella Boom says:** "If you gotta take notes just to prove your feelings, run, sis."

TERM	DEFINITION
Breadcrumbing	Giving tiny bits of attention to keep you hooked without real commitment. *Translation:* They text "hey stranger" every two weeks but can't plan a date. **Zephyr Blaze says:** "Don't chase crumbs when you were born to feast!"
Projection	When someone accuses you of what they're actually doing. *Translation:* They say you're being "too sensitive" while dodging accountability. **Sir Katticus says:** "If they keep handing you the mirror, they might be hiding their own mess."
Deflection	Redirecting blame to avoid responsibility. *Translation:* You bring up how they hurt you, and somehow, you're apologizing. **Nixie Starfire says:** "They can't own it? Don't rent them space in your peace."

TERM	DEFINITION
Toxic Blame-Shifting	Consistently blaming others to avoid the mirror. *Translation:* They break the vase, but suddenly it's your fault for placing it there. **Solana says:** "If you're always the villain in their stories, close the book."
Playing The Victim	They hurt you, then cry louder than you. *Translation:* You set a boundary, and suddenly you're the mean one. **Zephyr Blaze says:** "They skipped accountability and enrolled in Drama 101."

Healing Terms

The Language of Liberation

These are the words that wrapped you in grace and guided you home.

TERM	DEFINITION
Cocooning	A sacred season of rest, solitude, and transformation. *Translation:* It's not isolation. It's restoration. **Solana says:** "Don't rush your roots. The bloom is coming."

TERM	DEFINITION
Empath	A soul who feels everything, deeply and without filter. *Translation:* You cry during commercials and hold pain that isn't even yours. **Nixie Starfire says:** "Being soft in a sharp world? That's power, baby."
Glow-Up	The internal upgrade that eventually shows on the outside. *Translation:* You healed, hydrated, set boundaries, and it shows. **Bella Boom says:** "It's not about looking good for them. It's about feeling divine for you."
Chrysalis Season	The quiet, messy middle between who you were and who you're becoming. *Translation:* The world doesn't see it yet, but you're becoming magic. **Sir Katticus says:** "Transformation doesn't announce itself. It emerges."

TERM	DEFINITION
Soft Return	When joy sneaks back in after grief like morning light after storm clouds. *Translation:* Healing didn't roar. It whispered, "You're safe now." **Zephyr Blaze says:** "It's the giggle after the breakdown. That's real joy."
Inner Garden	Your sacred space of peace, healing, and joy. *Translation:* Not everyone gets access. Especially not the ones who trampled it. **Solana says:** "I bloom behind gates now. And I keep the key."

About the Characters

Solana – The Becoming Butterfly

The Butterfly. Represents the reader, the survivor, the woman learning to reclaim her glow. She's you. The one who didn't just survive the storm, she studied it, alchemized it, and now paints the sky with her wings. Her story is your mirror, your memory, your momentum.

- ➤ Theme: Resilience, Radiance, Reclamation
- ➤ Mantra: "I am not who I was, I'm who I dared to become."
- ➤ Role: The survivor, the healer, the rising soul
- ➤ Journal Spark: When did you last surprise yourself with your own strength?

Croix – The Masked Mirror

Smooth. Charming. Familiar. The Chameleon. A mirror of the narcissist, the shapeshifter, the toxic pattern. Croix is every lesson wrapped in temptation. He's the past that calls just when you've found peace. But make no mistake, he's a teacher. A test. A turning point. And when Solana rises, he fades.

- ➢ Theme: Illusion, Projection, False Closure
- ➢ Catchphrase: "I came to make it right," (But she already made peace.)
- ➢ Role: The ghost of the old pattern, the final exam, the reflection of what you've outgrown
- ➢ Journal Spark: What part of your past still tries to re-enter through sweet words and soft eyes?

Zephyr Blaze – The Spark That Says "More, Please!"

The sassy truth-teller in sequins. Stands for intuition, fire, and fierce clarity. Zephyr is joy in motion. That unapologetic friend who hypes your glow-up like it's the Grammy Awards. Loud, loyal, and the embodiment of freedom in your full expression.

- ➢ Theme: Celebration, Visibility, Hype
- ➢ Catchphrase: "Baby, you didn't come this far to blend. You came to set it off."
- ➢ Role: Your cheerleader, joy coach, and truth-delivering jester
- ➢ Journal Spark: Where in your life do you need a louder cheer section?

Bella Boom – The Queen of Boundaries & Beauty

The embodied diva of boundaries. Stomps in truth. Swings joy like a bat. Bella doesn't play about worth. She reminds you that "No" is a full sentence, and that self-love can wear heels and hoop earrings. She's the guardian of your peace, and she'll do it with a wink.

> ➤ Theme: Boundaries, Confidence, Divine Femininity
> ➤ Catchphrase: "They don't get access just because they apologize. This is healed-girl pricing now."
> ➤ Role: The sass with class, the line-drawer, the mirror of your worth
> ➤ Journal Spark: Where do you need to tighten your energetic guest list?

Sir Katticus Flame – The Silent Seer with a Mean Side-Eye

The soulful philosopher. Slow-sipping wisdom, always in a velvet robe. Wise. Observant. Doesn't waste words, but when he speaks, it lands. Sir Katticus is your instinct, the one who felt the shift in the room before the words even dropped.

> ➤ Theme: Inner Wisdom, Protection, Intuition
> ➤ Catchphrase: "If the vibe shifts, trust the shift. Don't gaslight your gut."
> ➤ Role: The guardian, the intuitive, the shade-throwing sage

> ➢ Journal Spark: When was the last time you ignored your inner knowing, and what did it cost you?

Nixie Starfire – The Soul Whisperer

Half glitter, half grit. The cosmic whisperer reminding you of your divine magic. Nixie is your soft knowing. The healer voice inside you that doesn't scream, it glows. She shows up in your stillness, your prayers, your poetry. She is your divinity in motion.

> ➢ Theme: Grace, Healing, Divine Feminine Flow
> ➢ Catchphrase: "You're not being tested to go back, you're being shown how far you've come."
> ➢ Role: Your spiritual compass, your softness, your sacred whisper
> ➢ Journal Spark: What has your soul been trying to tell you lately, beneath the noise?

This lounge isn't fiction. It's a mirror.

Every character is a piece of your journey.

Every voice is one you've needed.

And now?

You get to decide who stays in your garden.

Your Soul Circle Awaits and now, It's Your Turn

Soul-Cast & Inner Lounge Worksheet

Instructions: This is your creative lounge, where the voices, characters, and parts of you gather.

Write, doodle, color, or decorate. There are no wrong answers.

1. Who's in Your Lounge?

List every "inner character" that shows up in your life, real or imagined.

_____

_____

_____

_____

_____

2. Final Spark: Who is in your soul-cast?

The main characters in your life story, the ones who shape your journey.

_____

_____

_____

_____

_____

3. Write their names. Draw them. Channel them.

(Use the space below to write or sketch their essence.)

_____

_____

_____

_____

_____

4. What characters live inside you?

_____

_____

_____

_____

_____

5. Who's the voice that hypes you up?

_____

_____

_____

_____

_____

6. Who sets the boundary?

_____

_____

_____

_____

_____

7. Who heals in silence?

_____

_____

_____

_____

_____

8. And who are you becoming?

_____

_____

_____

_____

_____

This is your soul circle, your constellation of becoming.
Name them. Honor them. Let them speak.
And protect your circle like the sanctuary it is.

Character Lounge: Relationship Green & Red Flags

Where wisdom meets wit, and your favorite crew speaks the truth about love, boundaries, and the fine art of not settling.

As Told by the Crew:

Zephyr Blaze, Bella Boom, Sir Katticus Flame, Nixie Starfire... and Solana

Theme: Love that Heals vs. Love that Hijacks
Setting: Solana's Sanctuary, Mid-Morning with Truth Tea

Solana was curled up in her sunroom sipping lavender tea, surrounded by journals, jazz, and a few truth-tellers who knew their way around a red flag like GPS.

"Let's talk about it," she said, flipping open a notebook labeled *What I Won't Settle for Again.*

The crew nodded in divine agreement.

Solana closes her journal and smiles:
"I used to collect red flags like souvenirs. Now? I plant green ones like seeds. If it doesn't grow me, glow me, or ground me... it can't stay."

Moral

Love shouldn't feel like a scavenger hunt for decency.
The right one won't make your peace a negotiation or your glow a threat.
May your next love be soft, sacred, and sure.

Green Flags – The "Yes, Honey!" Edition

SIGNAL (WHAT TO LOOK FOR)	PULL QUOTE
They Respect Your Boundaries Without Making It a Debate.	*"If they don't flinch when you say no, that's not just powerful and spiritual, it's sacred alignment."* *– Nixie Starfire*
They Cheer for Your Glow; Even When They Are Not the Source.	*"If they don't need to dim your light to feel seen? Baby, that's a whole sunrise with Wi-Fi."* *– Zephyr Blaze*
They Apologize and Adjust; Not Just Apologize and Repeat.	*"If 'I'm sorry' comes with changed behavior? That's not just growth; that's divine reciprocity and foreplay."* *– Bella Boom*
They're Consistent, Not Just Convenient.	*"A real one shows up when it's cloudy, not just when your sunshine's on sale."* *– Sir Katticus Flame*
They See Your Scars and Don't Flinch.	*"If they honor the journey that made you radiant? That's love, not projection."* *"You don't have to shrink to be safe."* *"If your softness is celebrated; not studied for weakness; you've found peace in human form."* *– Solana*

Red Flags – The "Run, Don't Recycle" Edition

PATTERN (WHAT TO WATCH OUT FOR)	PULL QUOTE
They Ghost You… And Call It "Space."	"If disappearing is their love language, block them in all dialects; including Morse code." – Nixie Starfire
They Only Show Up When You're Glowing but Were Mia During the Grieving.	"If they skipped your shadow work but pop up for the sparkle? Return to sender. That's a glitter chaser, not a partner." – Zephyr Blaze
They Call You "Too Much" Right After They Emptied Your Cup.	"If loving you drains them; let 'em hydrate elsewhere. Your love is not a drought relief fund." – Bella Boom
You Feel Like a Therapist with Benefits.	"If you're doing all the emotional labor, baby; you're not in love, you're in customer service." – Sir Katticus Flame
You Shrink Around Them and Call It "Compromise."	"If your glow gets quiet in their presence? That's not alignment; it's erosion." – Solana

Q&A for the Soul

- Which of these flags, green or red, has shown up in your past relationships?

_____

_____

_____

_____

_____

- Are you accepting consistency or clinging to chemistry?

_____

_____

_____

_____

- When was the last time someone honored your "no" without protest or persuasion?

_____

_____

_____

_____

_____

- How do you show up as a green flag?

_____

_____

_____

_____

_____

Writing Challenge

Write a love letter to your future relationship.

- Describe how it feels, not just how it looks.

_____

_____

_____

_____

_____

- What boundaries exist? What does mutual respect sound like?

_____

_____

_____

_____

_____

- How are you different in this version of love?

_____

_____

_____

_____

_____

Journal Prompts

- "What Does Love Feel Like When It's Safe?"

_____

_____

_____

_____

_____

- Write about a moment, real or imagined, when you felt completely accepted, not for what you could do, fix, or prove, but simply for who you are.

_____

_____

_____

_____

_____

- What did your body feel like in that space?

_____

_____

_____

_____

_____

- What was missing that you'd grown used to tolerating?

_____

_____

_____

_____

- What did presence, not performance, look like?

_____

_____

_____

_____

- Then ask yourself:
  What boundaries would I need to keep that kind of peace sacred?

_____

_____

_____

_____

Affirmations

- ➤ I don't audition for love.
- ➤ I attract what aligns.
- ➤ I attract what honors me.
- ➤ I choose love that nourishes, not depletes.
- ➤ My glow does not require shrinking, proving, or pain.
- ➤ My peace is the gatekeeper.
- ➤ My heart is the garden and only those who tend, not trample, may enter.

Bonus: The "Joy Glow" Playlist

Songs that hold you while you heal, and hype you while you rise.

CHAPTER	THEME	SONG	WHY IT RESONATES
1	Hiding / Survival	*"Lost One"* – Jazmine Sullivan	Painful honesty and emotional reckoning
1	Hiding / Survival	*"Elastic Heart"* – Sia	Fighting spirit wrapped in vulnerability
1	Hiding / Survival	*"Rise Up"* – Andra Day	A soul-deep anthem for resilience
2	Adapting to Please	*"I Choose"* – India.Arie	Gentle reclaiming of identity
2	Adapting to Please	*"Try"* – Colbie Caillat	Letting go of perfection and masks
3	Boundaries	*"Masterpiece"* – Jazmine Sullivan	Owning your worth as both art and author

CHAPTER	THEME	SONG	WHY IT RESONATES
3	Boundaries	*"Respect"* – Aretha Franklin	The unapologetic demand for dignity
4	Reclaiming Self	*"Roar"* – Katy Perry	The moment your voice breaks through
4	Reclaiming Self	*"I Am Light"* – India.Arie	Remembering your essence beyond mistakes
5	Letting Go	*"Bag Lady"* – Erykah Badu	What we carry and what we need to drop
5	Letting Go	*"Let It Be"* – The Beatles	Surrender as a form of peace
6	True Glow-Up	*"Cranes in the Sky"* – Solange	Healing is quiet, slow, and sacred
6	True Glow-Up	*"Unstoppable"* – Sia	Quiet strength that turns into undeniable power
7	Light Switch Lies	*"Love Yourself"* – Mary J. Blige	You shine when you choose yourself
7	Light Switch Lies	*"No Scrubs"* – TLC	Playful but clear boundaries
8	Joy Reclaimed	*"Good Days"* – SZA	Reflection, peace, and healing joy

CHAPTER	THEME	SONG	WHY IT RESONATES
8	Joy Reclaimed	*"Walking on Sunshine"* – Katrina & The Waves	Joy in its purest, most unfiltered form
9	Inner Peace	*"Golden"* – Jill Scott	The anthem of living free and full
9	Inner Peace	*"Lovely Day"* – Bill Withers	Choosing light every morning
10	Anthem of Power	*"I'm Every Woman"* – Chaka Khan	She. Doesn't. Blend. Anymore.
10	Anthem of Power	*"Run the World (Girls)"* – Beyoncé	Power without Apology

Acknowledgements

To the ones who saw me before I ever saw myself, thank you. To every person who's ever doubted their worth, dimmed their light, or stayed too long in places that couldn't hold their wings, this is for you. You gave me the courage to write what needed to be said, to feel what had long been buried, and to rise in the truth of my becoming.

To my son, my heart with feet, your love is a compass. Watching you grow gave me the bravery to unlearn everything that told me I had to shrink. You reminded me that wings are inherited through healing.

To my ancestors, known and unknown, who endured what I cannot imagine so I could stand here in this sacred glow. I feel your prayers pressed into the pages.

To my tribe: the sisters, soul-friends, and sacred mirrors who held space for my tears, my mess, my silence, and my return. Your encouragement wrapped around me like sunlight in the dark.

To the mentors and editors who sharpened my voice without dulling my spirit, your wisdom was a lantern. Thank you for honoring both the poet and the warrior in me.

To everyone who whispered, "I needed this," after a workshop, retreat, or post, your words were the breadcrumbs back to my purpose. This book is my love letter to your healing.

To God, the Creator, the Great Weaver of stories, thank you for trusting me with this one.

And finally, to the little girl I used to be… who thought her survival was something to be ashamed of. You didn't just survive, you alchemized. This book is your voice, unmuted.

Sources & Suggested Reading

A field guide for curious souls, deep feelers,
and wisdom seekers

T he journey through survival, self-reclamation, and soulful transformation is stitched together not only by our lived experiences, but also by the wisdom, research, and inspiration of those who came before us. These pages sing because of the voices that whispered behind them.

Below are a few texts, studies, and stories that helped shape this book's wings, and might help shape yours too.

On Emotional Healing & Transformation

- ➤ *The Body Keeps the Score* by Bessel van der Kolk
- ➤ *Women Who Run with the Wolves* by Clarissa Pinkola Estés

➢ *Untamed* by Glennon Doyle

➢ *Radical Acceptance* by Tara Brach

➢ *Homecoming: Reclaiming and Championing Your Inner Child* by John Bradshaw

On Narcissism, Gaslighting & Trauma Recovery

➢ *Psychopath Free* by Jackson MacKenzie

➢ *Will I Ever Be Free of You?* by Karyl McBride

➢ *Healing from Hidden Abuse* by Shannon Thomas

➢ *The Gaslight Effect* by Dr. Robin Stern

On Personal Growth & Empowerment

➢ *Becoming* by Michelle Obama

➢ *The Gifts of Imperfection* by Brené Brown

➢ *Big Magic* by Elizabeth Gilbert

➢ *Set Boundaries, Find Peace* by Nedra Glover Tawwab

➢ *Sacred Woman* by Queen Afua

➢ *Atlas of the Heart* by Brené Brown

On Butterflies, Metamorphosis & Nature's Wisdom

➢ National Geographic – Butterfly Life Cycle Studies

➢ Smithsonian Institution – "Butterflies and Moths of North America"

- ➤ "Chameleons: Masters of Disguise" – BBC Wildlife Documentary
- ➤ *The Metamorphosis* by Franz Kafka (for metaphorical inspiration)

> *These works walked beside me as I wrote.*
> *Let them walk beside you as you rise.*

With love and wings,

Volari Morgan

Backstage
Pass

Sneak Peek: The Next Season

We have walked through storms, shed old skins, and discovered what it means to rise again with wings stronger than before. But here is the truth: growth does not stay neatly tucked away in our personal lives. It spills into boardrooms, break rooms, and every space where people gather to work, lead, and follow.

This is your backstage pass, an invitation to step behind the curtain with me. Not into a theater, but into the workplace, where roles, masks, and performances can be just as demanding. Here, the lessons of resilience, empathy, and self-worth are put to the test in real time.

This is also your sneak peek into the next season, a glimpse of what happens when healing and transformation meet the world of leadership. Because the butterfly does not only fly in private. She shows up in meetings, in conflict, and in the way she carries herself when the pressure is high.

The workplace is one of the greatest stages of transformation. It is where collaboration collides with conflict, where ambition can fuel creativity or destroy trust, and where leadership is revealed not by title, but by how you treat the people who look to you for guidance.

The next season is about courage in action. It is about asking the challenging questions no one else will ask. It is about learning to hold boundaries without losing compassion. It is about shifting from surviving systems to reshaping them. It is about protecting your wings in environments that do not always value softness, empathy, or truth. This is leadership with soul, leadership that breathes, leadership that remembers the human before the task.

I will leave you with a moment, a scene from behind the curtain, where courage whispered louder than silence.

A Lesson in Leadership

Leadership is not about titles or authority. It is about presence; how you make others feel in your company, and how you stand in your truth when the room grows tense.

A Workplace Moment

The conference room was still.
Not peaceful. Not calm.
But heavy.

The kind of silence you can feel pressing against your chest.

A dozen of us sat around a polished table, papers spread like shields. Pens tapped. Chairs squeaked. The hum of the air vent was louder than anyone's voice. And then the words landed:

"Beginning next quarter, workloads will double. No additional resources."

The announcement echoed like a stone hitting water, pulling the room down with it. Eyes dropped. Throats tightened. Some scribbled on paper, not because there was anything to write, but because it was safer than being seen.

Inside me, a battle rose. My pulse quickened. My throat burned. Stay quiet, a voice warned. Do not rock the boat. Do not draw fire.

But then another voice, softer, steadier, almost ancestral.
You know silence does not protect you. It only prolongs the pain.

So, I inhaled. Slow. Steady.
I raised my hand.

And with a voice I barely recognized as my own, I asked the question…

And here, we pause.

Because leadership does not always arrive with grand speeches. It enters in small questions, in steady presence, in the choice to speak when silence grows too heavy.

This is only the beginning of what it looks like when the butterfly walks into the boardroom. The rest of the story will unfold in the next season.

Final Teaser

The next season is not about titles.
It is about truth, about courage, about the air you change when you walk into the room.

Coming soon: leadership with soul, with strategy, with wings strong enough to shift the culture around you.

This is not the end.
It is the opening scene of a new story…
the butterfly in the boardroom.

About the Author

*V*olari Morgan is a passionate author, transformational coach, and multi-hyphenate visionary whose work bridges empowerment, healing, and heart. She is the celebrated author of *Shifted Masterpiece: A Story of Love & Horror in Savannah, GA* and now, *Chameleons and Butterflies* She is the founder of **Joy Glow**, a wellness brand that creates sacred spaces for women to reclaim their voice, power, and joy.

In addition to her literary work, she is also the founder of a mission-driven non-profit organization dedicated to personal development, advocacy, and community resilience. With a heart rooted in service and a mind sharpened by strategy, the former math and science educator is equipped with over three decades of professional experiences and serves as a respected leader in corporate America.

Whether guiding a retreat, mentoring women, writing by candlelight, or leading transformation inside Fortune 500 walls, she lives by one mission: **to ignite the light in others, until they remember it was never gone.**

Invite Me to Speak or Lead

Let's turn inspiration into transformation, together.

If you're planning a retreat, conference, school event, corporate training, women's circle, or community workshop, I'd be honored to join you. I speak from the soul and lead with purpose, infusing every moment with energy, empathy, and empowerment.

Topics I speak and teach on:

- Healing & Transformation
- Reclaiming Your Voice & Power
- Emotional Intelligence & Resilience
- Faith & Fierce Self-Love
- Leadership, Purpose & Vision
- Self-Care That Actually Heals
- Writing as a Sacred Practice
- Surviving Narcissistic & Toxic Relationships
- Joy in the Workplace: Mindfulness & Meaning in Corporate Life

> ➢ Founder's Journey: From Nonprofit to CEO of Joy Glow

Formats include:

- ➢ Keynotes & Panels
- ➢ Workshops & Retreats
- ➢ Book Clubs & Reading Circles
- ➢ Podcast Guesting & Virtual Talks
- ➢ Youth & School Programming
- ➢ Faith-Based Gatherings
- ➢ Executive & Leadership Training

To inquire about availability, honorarium, and booking:

Visit http://www.myjoyglows.com/speaking
or email contact@myjoyglows.com

Book & Joy Glow Inquiries

*H*ave a question about the book? Want to share your story or invite me to join your circle?

I love connecting with readers, facilitators, and healing-centered spaces. Whether you're interested in bulk orders, hosting a healing circle, or just want to send love, I'd love to hear from you.

Let's build something beautiful together.

- ➤ Book Clubs & Bulk Orders
- ➤ Custom Retreat Journals or Healing Toolkits
- ➤ Media & Podcast Inquiries
- ➤ Joy Glow Collaborations
- ➤ General Questions & Reader Reflections

Reach out directly at **contact@myjoyglows.com**

or visit **www.myjoyglows.com**

More by the Author

Explore more soulful stories and healing adventures by the author of Chameleons and Butterflies.

Painted Wings & Patchy Tails: Too Fancy for the Mud

A laugh-out-loud, heartwarming fable for children (and the grown-ups who love them). Follow Patchy the fashion-forward chameleon and Bella the Butterfly Queen as they learn that true magic comes from within, even when you're stuck in the mud. Full of rhymes, giggles, and journal prompts, this playful tale blends emotional wisdom with whimsical wonder.

Perfect for ages 5+, classrooms, family reading, and young hearts learning big lessons. Stay tuned, it's coming soon.

Shifted Masterpiece: A Story of Love & Horror in Savannah, GA

Set in the hauntingly beautiful backdrop of Savannah, this raw, powerful, and riveting story traces one woman's catastrophic secret, one man's unleashed obsession, and one terrifyingly true story. When it comes to love and family, *Shifted Masterpiece* is a mind-blowing testimony filled with cringeworthy and unforeseen truths.

Trigger warning: This book includes mature themes and is intended for adult readers seeking healing, honesty, and hope.

***

Whether you're reading with your inner child or healing your whole self, these books will meet you in the mud, in the mystery, and in the masterpiece.

To purchase or learn more, visit **bit.ly/shiftedmasterpiecebook**

Notes

Notes

Notes

Notes

Notes

Notes

Notes

Notes

Notes

Notes

Notes

Notes

Notes

Notes

Notes

Notes

Notes

Notes

Notes

Notes

Notes

Notes

Notes

Notes

Notes

Notes

Notes

Notes

Notes

Notes

Notes

Notes

Notes

Notes

Notes

Notes

Notes

Notes

Notes

Notes

www.ingramcontent.com/pod-product-compliance
Lightning Source LLC
Chambersburg PA
CBHW021217130626
46554CB00004B/1255